# GOD'S INNER CIRCLE

# GOD'S INNER CIRCLE

## The Radical Devotion of Elie Wiesel to Faith

### A SEEKER'S SCRAPBOOK OF QUOTATIONS

ᔓ

*Compilation and Commentary*
MICHAEL RITZEN

KTAV PUBLISHING HOUSE, INC.
2012

Copyright © 2012 Michael Ritzen

Published by
KTAV Publishing House, Inc.
888 Newark Avenue, Suite 119
Jersey City, NJ 07306
orders@ktav.com <mailto:orders@ktav.com>
(201) 963-9524

Library of Congress Cataloging-in-Publication Data

Ritzen, Michael.
    God's inner circle : the radical devotion of Elie Wiesel to faith : a seeker's
scrapbook of quotations / compilation and commentary, Michael Ritzen.
        p.   cm.
    ISBN 978-1-60280-211-7
    1. Wiesel, Elie, 1928—Quotations.   2. Faith (Judaism)—Quotations, maxims,
etc.   3. Holocaust, Jewish (1939-1945)—Moral and ethical aspects—Quotations,
maxims, etc.   I. Wiesel, Elie, 1928–   II. Title.
PQ2683.I32Z855   1982
813'.54—dc23
                                                                2012015989

# Dedications

Kathryn—My wife of fifty years. My partner for fifty-four. My . . . everything (Everything).

The Whippoorwill's lament deepens his song of love.

Noah Frost—Our son: brave, earnest, loving, constant source of deep pride. Beloved.

Sandra Krasner—My word-processor: Indispensable mistress of the internet, design and professional support. Her mantra: "Don't worry, I can do it." And how! True heart. A blessing.

# Personal Acknowledgments

Rabbi Robert Sternberg—Retired Director of the Hatikvah Holocaust Education Center of Springfield, Mass.

For your generous, unqualified and enthusiastic support.

Beth Perlman—Professional Reader: Early and helpful, objective, editorial feedback.

Ruth Alcabes—Librarian and thorough research skills.

Hilton Abbott—Dear friend. Dedicated Motivational Coach and tireless technical advisor/facilitator.

Without you this would still be in draft #9

Mr. Bernard Scharfstein—Publisher Supreme. Encouragement? Abundant. Patience? Beyond words. Vision? Wise and true. Definition? Mensch Extraordinaire. Conclusion? My gratitude runneth over. . . .

## Who Is Elie Wiesel and What Can He Teach Me?

Foremost among well-known Holcaust survivors, as spokesperson, lecturer, professor, witness, world figure . . . stands Elie Wiesel. Author of fifty books. Nobel Peace Laureate. As an observant Jew, a most predictable question arises following his public lectures: "In the face of your God's failure to save six million Holocaust victims, how can you still embrace belief?" This monograph is an attempt to gather, organize, discuss and honor a selection of his multiple responses, his theodicy as developed over seventy years.

Wiesel's specific words are known to provoke, anger, inspire, puzzle, and for some, enrapture listeners and readers of all religions and those of no religion at all. Central to this endeavor remains the classic memoir, *NIGHT*. In it, as a teen-age camp prisoner Wiesel experienced his God, once believed to be omnipotent, now dying on the Auschwitz gallows. If your curiosity calls— answer it by considering the upcoming contents and two-page Introduction. May this scrapbook of quotations provide you the precise words able to help formulate and to illuminate religious insights and the hard-won wisdom you continually seek. . . .

## Who Is the Author and Why Should I Read Him?

If you've never read words written by someone born in Butte, Montana and raised in Fargo, North Dakota, by Russian immigrant Orthodox Jewish grandparents . . . you just did. Approaching Bar Mitzvah age necessitated move to Minnesota and what became a spiritual adoption by the Minneapolis Talmud Torah Academy. Eventual Valedictorian of the Advanced Study class of 1953. An experimental single year of solo living in Boston, MA. became ten years of searching Employment Ads, entering and withdrawing from Brandeis and various other colleges, religious turmoil, psychotherapy and somehow a lucky marriage in 1962.

Returned to the University of Minnesota to complete a B.A. (Summa Cum Laude) and M.A. (National Defense Education Act Fellowship). Age thirty-five adopted Noah (named after the biblical Noah). Poetry published in Best College Verse, Jewish Digest, and other journals now defunct. Hired as Professor of English at Springfield Technical Community College in Massachusetts. Created and lectured on weekly radio "Heat and Power Poetry Hour." Initiated and taught classes on Literature of the Holocaust. Also guest speaker at Orthodox to Reform synagogues on "Confessions of a Marginal Jew," "The Edge of Holiness" (with liberal quotation from Elie Wiesel) and on Jewish humor. After retirement from thirty years of college teaching, time became available to prepare this more personal than "academic" thesis based on Elie Wiesel's radical and sometimes fierce devotion to God.

**Boston University**

Elie Wiesel
*University Professor and*
*Andrew W. Mellon Professor in the Humanities*

147 Bay State Road
Boston, Massachusetts 02215
617-353-4561 Fax: 617-353-4024

June 12, 2007

Professor Michael Ritzen
32 Belleclaire Avenue
Longmeadow, MA 01106

Dear Professor Ritzen,

Have I answered you yet? If not, please forgive the delay!

In any case, as you can imagine I was moved, reading the extended essay you developed on my work. The theme of faith that is at the center of your monograph is also at the center of my life. As you understand, all questions must remain open....

Simply: thank you for your gift...and my congratulations on your retirement—

With every good wish,

*Elie Wiesel*

# Contents

# Introduction

M ANY OF US POST-HOLOCAUST JEWS and nonJews sur- prise ourselves at our dubious ability to balance doubts about a living and/or loving God with our public and private prayers. They resonate as though the Holocaust never happened. Prayers with one eye closed. We seem unable to let go of Him.

Is there a way for us to maintain this precarious see-saw of doubt and devotion with honesty and integrity if not grace? Probably not. But Elie Wiesel does so with considerable authority and often with compelling eloquence. Why Wiesel? Because as one of the earliest and most prolific Holocaust survivors both willing and able to articulate the dilemmas of post-Holocaust belief, he has dedicated his life to preserving the memory, the nightmare of Auschwitz, and thus the ensuing struggles with belief in man and in God which those memories ignite. Even detractors concede his many tales and essays comprise a virtual "testament to the ages." Wiesel's fundamental belief in God has remained steadfast with generous allowance for doubts, wounds, fury, quarrels and prayers. Prayers, that is, with both eyes open. His words:

God is involved in man's destiny—good or bad. To thank Him for Jerusalem and not question Him for Treblinka is hypocrisy. (—as quoted in *What Jews Say About God*, A.J. Kolatch, Ed. 206)

One intention of this monograph is to trace how that questioning of Treblinka ("Where was God?") did not end in divorce from his apparently absent God, if not also from Judaism itself. In Wiesel's own words. The Temple doors to secular Judaism have welcomed many who "questioned Him on Treblinka" only to receive the same silence. Why, in other words, does Wiesel repeat the tale which ends this study in which war-torn Jews continue to sing their traditional prayers but so softly, so fearfully, in order not to reveal their hiding place from the punishing God in whom they still believed.

What follows is an idiosyncratic sampling of some of his relevant quotations. They may provoke, annoy, anger, haunt and sometimes deeply move. For some, struggling with the same questions, they have been known to help. My selections are not chronological, nor do they claim completeness. Sources include novels, essays, tales, memoirs, interviews, lectures, confessions. Topic headings can sometimes seem arbitrary since a few quotations answer to more than one subject. Readers may also discover additional quotations, missing here, which amplify or contradict my choices. Wiesel often claims he is no systematic theologian but "merely a teller of tales."

As for the claim "radical devotion," he would likely cringe and point out that everything he has written about God has been said or implied in *Job*, other holy scriptures, Talmud, folklore, work of his Chassidic masters, theologians, etc. What seems "radical" (that is: to the root, basic, drastic, extreme, daring) to some can be mainstream to others and often irrelevant to the rest. No argument. To borrow one of his favorite expressions, "and yet," millions have found that Wiesel speaks in a voice haunting, penetrating, like no one else. We need him. What follows, therefore, is a collection of Wiesel's thoughts, his agony and his fierceness of faith, in a new sequence that suggests the development of a radical devotion in the writings of one seminal, post-Holocaust Jew.

# Prologue

To be a Jew is to have all the reasons in the world not to have faith in language, in singing, in prayers, and in God, but to go on telling the tale, to go on carrying on the dialogue, and to have my own silent prayers and quarrels with God. (Wiesel quoted in Roth and Berenbaum 369).

A one sentence distillation of Wieselian faith that sets the tone and direction of many entries that follow. It will be examined more closely in the section "God's Inner Circle."

The Holocaust has forced all Jews to rethink our principles, customs, beliefs. It has made us more and less devoted. But something happened: it didn't leave anyone unchanged. . . . (Freedman 32).

Nor unchallenged, we might add. Jew and nonJew. Victim and observer. Generation one, two, three. As for survivors, Wiesel divides them thus:

[The survivor] could say: I have suffered, I have been made to suffer, all I can do is draw closer to my own people. And that was understandable. Or else: I have suffered too much, I have no strength left, I withdraw, I do not wish my children to inherit this suffering. And that, too, was understandable (*A Jew Today* 15).

To "draw closer" to one's own people, of course, need not involve a belief in God. Conversely, one may withdraw from Jewish identity and yet maintain such a belief. Our focus, however, leads to what Wiesel calls "The Drama of the Believer" who identifies as a Jew.

Prominent among all the philosophers, theologians and scholars who have written on post-Holocaust theology is the prolific, controversial, and late Emil Fackenheim. In his slim volume *God's Presence in History*, which is dedicated to Elie Wiesel, one finds this declaration: "[Elie Wiesel's] writings are forcing Jewish theological thought in our time into a new dimension." Fackenheim would likely agree that his "new dimension" is not exclusive to Jewish theological thought. Professor Josephine Knopp, in the final sentence of her article "Wiesel and the Absurd" opens that dimension considerably:

Ivan Karamazov believes that without God all things are possible; Wiesel shares with us his discovery that all things are possible even with God and therein lies his unique contribution to our understanding of the human condition (Cargas 100).

# Night

Wiesel often claimed that the seeds for all his writing (now fifty plus books) can be found in his first work, *Night*, written in his late 20's. A memoir, it covers the years in Auschwitz and Buchenwald, ages 15 to 17. The book, a classic, often assigned in high schools and colleges, has been read more than any similar testimony (Ann Frank's diary ends before her internment.). By age 15, Wiesel was deeply religious and devout. He loved Torah, Chassidic lore, and he loved God. The following passages from *Night*, often quoted, challenge those convictions so profoundly that their recovery—no—that the coming to terms with faith initiates and then becomes his lifelong struggle. Forget "God's Inner Circle." For now, the destination even to "God's Outer Circle" may still be up for debate. Nevertheless, for many, Wiesel remains the authentic pathfinder. . .

The camp: Buna (called Auschwitz 3). Year: 1943. Occasion: Public Hanging. Two men and a young boy. In front of thousands of prisoners. They were forced to march past the hanging corpses.

> Only the two adults were no longer alive. . . . But the third rope was still moving; being so light, the child was still alive. . . . Behind me, I heard . . . "Where is God now?" and I heard a voice within me answer him: "Where is He? Here He is—He is hanging here on the gallows." . . . That night the soup tasted of corpses (65).

The conclusion of Chapter 4, from which these lines were taken, according to Michael Morgan in his study of Post-Holocaust theology, *Beyond Auschwitz*, "is probably the most recalled and cited episode in all Holocaust literature; for in it is raised the idea that the death camps were a radical break in life and thought, not for the victims alone but for all of us, and that to go on requires going on in a different way" (33).

Many read the episode as declaring the death of God. Wiesel regrets this misinterpretation which he claims "borders on blasphemy." If indeed blasphemy, it is one in which he perhaps momentarily and anomalously participates earlier in the chapter upon first viewing the flames which consume the bodies of children: "Never shall I forget those moments which murdered my God and my soul and turned my dreams to dust" (34). Other readers of the hanging scene, who see the gasping child as a sign of God likely view Him as still alive but weak, helpless and possibly suffering for His people. Alternatively, He may not appear to all as merely helpless, but rather as symbolically "dying" by way of refusal to interfere with natural consequences of man's free will. It is conceivably more in the hearts of some traditional believers (like young Elie) in whom the perception of a once omnipotent and merciful Jehovah is in danger of, if not death, than of necessitating a possibly traumatic new understanding of His mysterious will and questionable powers.

Regarding the child: does he represent Everyman? No, replies the author, he is a particular man—a particular Jew. Does he then represent Jesus? Emphatically not Wiesel's intention. And what of the "voice within me" claiming God "is here on the gallows?" Wiesel at Amherst College in a 1976 lecture responded that it "may be the voice of God. Maybe . . . maybe not, but maybe." Although final consensus on these questions "must await the Messiah," Wiesel reconsiders the issue when he addresses "What About My Faith?" following Stage IV (p. 87).

In spite of such overwhelming and incomprehensible despair, a scattering of prisoners, some Jews, some outspoken Christians, some resolute Jehovah's Witnesses, some gypsies and even some quasi-atheists, managed to pray and attempt religious observance. Thus, the quandary: how must already starving Jewish men and women fulfill the usual requirement to fast on Yom Kippur, the holiest day on the Jewish calendar? Indeed, Jewish law sanctions the preservation of life above all obligations and restrictions. Young Elie had other thoughts: ". . . There was no longer any reason why I should fast. I no longer accepted God's silence. As I swallowed my soup, I saw in the gesture an act of rebellion and protest against Him" (69). And what of those who did in fact fast on the Holy Days but only as an act of protest? How so? They fasted and thereby honored the covenant, but most remarkably they justified having done so only "to shame Him" (*Legends* 61; more on this in STAGE II).

Coincidentally, these God-obsessed, heart-breaking (and to

some, "Absurd") dramas of religious rebellion were occurring contemporaneously with the attempts of Albert Camus in the early 1940s to articulate his own secular existential definition of "The Absurd." The "Final Solution" (genocide of the Jews) became official Nazi policy in 1942, the year Camus published *The Myth of Sisyphus.* The Sisyphus of Greek legend whom he honors in the essay becomes the symbol and embodiment of rebellion against a meaningless, Godless and Absurd universe. He is the same Sisyphus who will keep appearing when least expected in these pages, to serve as a sounding board against which to contrast the usually God-centered "Absurd" experienced by the victims and survivors of "the Holocaust." How many miles, after all, separated Camus' study in Paris from Berlin, 1942, or his work in the French Resistance from an Auschwitz where rebels in a desperate world, mavens of existential absurdity transformed a mere cup of cold diluted soup into a weapon of protest against—and simultaneously an unintended offering of devotion to—their mysterious God?

The original metaphor of a God on the gallows, too weak to stay alive, and yet too light even to die is outrageous. But no more so than the conclusion drawn by an anonymous fellow prisoner of the narrator who reasoned that someone will fill the vacuum created by the absent, the defeated God and: "I've got more faith in Hitler than anyone else. He's the only one who's kept his promises, all his promises, to the Jewish people" (77). So far, at least in *Night*, so true. . . .

Wiesel has submitted to innumerable interviews. Many of his responses are quoted here. One of the earliest was in conversation with the author and editor Harry James Cargas, which contains this stark and unequivocal declaration. It comes as no surprise: "I believe, during the Holocaust, the covenant was broken" (56). "Broken" for the duration of the Holocaust only or "broken" ever since? Either way, though many may disagree, this time the "guilty party," by implication, is not man.

God's failure to "enter history" and thereby stop the killings in Treblinka, douse the fires of Auschwitz, confirmed for many that regarding the biblical covenant between Himself and His People, time had run out. If God no longer honored His covenantal obligations, so too was man thereby released from his. Or so one would think. One, that is, unfamiliar with a selective "holy stubbornness" possessed by some Jews who argued in essence: "God or no God, we are bound by the vows of our ancestors and will continue to live by God's laws!" Believers in a living God, or a derelict God, or a dying God, or a possibly non-existent God, usually share at least two passions: to salvage what if any remains of value to them out of the broken covenant and, when necessary, when possible, to resolve (or surrender) their wounded relationships with God. Secular Jews from the start, unattached to a Source in which they believe or invest spiritual expectations, are spared this particular anguish. Wiesel was not so spared. Following the three background portraits of the next section, we commence the drama of Wiesel's complex fidelity to a God understood as Covenanter Who nevertheless failed, and not for the first time, to uphold His four thousand year commitment: the protection of His people from those who seek their annihilation. . . .

# Three Tales

## I. The Just Man of Sodom

S TATED SIMPLY, God's absence when his children face tor-
ture and death invalidates for many the ancient covenant
of loyalty and obedience in exchange for divine protection and
freedom. It need not, however, cancel personal morality. In *One
Generation After*, Wiesel tells of the "Just Man of Sodom" who
stood on street corners day and night preaching against sin and
debauchery. No one listened. After observing him many times
on his way to school, a child pulled at his robe and asked, "Why
do you go on and on every day when not even one person listens
to you?" He replied, "In the beginning, I thought I could change
man. Today I know I cannot. If I still shout today, if I still
scream, it is to prevent man from ultimately changing me" (72).
The Just Man has many brothers. One, the subject of this monograph, has stated in an interview, "I write because I must, and if
I still scream, it is to prevent the others from changing me."

## II. Sisyphus

A much earlier cousin is from Greek legend. Sources for the myth of Sisyphus can be found in Homer, where the heavens were busy with gods, spelled with a small "g". They were a lively group, capricious, jealous, vengeful, and their celestial and earthly playgrounds would appear to a monotheistic culture as Godless. Sisyphus was King of Corinth. Zeus, Ruler of the Heavens, felt betrayed by Sisyphus and sentenced him to Hades, where he must push a boulder to the top of a mountain, only to see it roll back down, and then repeat the task—for eternity. Sinai it was not. Albert Camus saw in this myth a metaphor for modern man in his struggle with a Godless Absurd universe. The Just Man's kinship with Sisyphus is dubious, but instructive. God or no God in Sodom, the Just Man rebels against lawlessness. No monotheistic God atop the Sisyphus mountain, yet the hero rebels against an absurd fate. Though both rebels are joined by a fierce sense of honesty to oneself, Sisyphus was doomed to a solitary fate. His passion was fed, not by the debaucheries of Sodom, but rather by the absurdities of what he saw as a meaningless universe. The tale, as interpreted by Camus, offers a useful contrast to the "vision" of Wiesel, who nevertheless honors Camus as a crucial influence. Sisyphus, sans covenant, sans God, sans hope, in an "absurd" universe devoid of inherent meaning, does find, through his punishment, however, rebellion and thus passion and joy. In this universe, as Camus states it, "without a Master" Sisyphus eventually grows to understand "that all is well" and the essay ends: "One must imagine Sisyphus happy" (91). Wiesel, bound inextricably, for better or worse, to his "Master" (thus for him an intrinsically *meaningful* universe) is also well acquainted with "passion and joy." He is not, although, the model one seeks for reassurance "that all is well" nor as an exponent for a secular version of existential happiness.

Earlier in the essay, Camus asks:

IS ONE . . . GOING TO TAKE UP THE HEART RENDING AND MARVELOUS WAGER OF THE ABSURD? . . . AT LAST MAN WILL AGAIN FIND THERE THE WINE OF THE ABSURD AND THE BREAD OF INDIFFERENCE ON WHICH HE FEEDS HIS GREATNESS (39).

It is a wager heroic rebels (especially the hungry and thirsty) must find hard to resist. Enter Sinai. Enter Jews. Enter the Covenant. Enter the Covenant shattered into more pieces than the Ten Commandments in a painting by Samuel Bak. Does Camus's "wager of the absurd" now live? With two crucial Wieselian updates. For Jews, the "Bread of Indifference" becomes the "Bread of Affliction" for those who died because they were Jews and who, tragically, absurdly, will never know if or how their lives are honored in the ensuing generations. As for "Wine of the Absurd," it is drunk at the birth of children, some of whom might one day fatally be discovered by racial purists as having even a trace of "impure Jewish blood." "Absurd" defiance. "Absurd" hope. "Absurd" beliefs in the influence of Survivor-Witness. Perhaps even "Absurd" delusions of God. It is *this* bitter wine and sour bread on which Jews feed their greatness. Sisyphus, at least, was free of ancient loyalty to an absent God. A luxury, Wiesel might say, that Jews cannot afford. Although Camus claims, "One must imagine Sisyphus happy," Wiesel would likely wish him well, but, due to his own non-negotionable belief in God, part company.

Meanwhile, meet the Fatman: a Chassid who, like Sisyphus, was a virtuoso in the craft of protest, a savant in the art of the Absurd. Like Sisyphus, he was cursed with a daunting weight, but the similarity may or may not end there. One can read his travail as a variation on the Sisyphian curse: heroic and futile. Believers, as we shall see, may contest the assertion of "futile. . . ."

## III. The Fatman

The Fatman lived alone in a small forest hut. One day, a rare knock at his door. It was the BESHT (Hebrew acronym for "Master of the Good Name"), a great eighteenth century religious leader and, some claim, founder of the Chassidic movement. When the door finally opened, the Besht was taken aback.

His host was obese, over 300 pounds, with food in his long beard, not to mention a manner so rude there was not even an unfriendly greeting. Silence. Leaving the door open, he shuffled back to his table and commenced eating. Gorging, to be more precise. The tiny room looked like the aftermath of a banquet, wine spilled, food everywhere, but none offered to the guest. The Besht entered, found a chair, and in silent astonishment, watched as the ravenous mouth devoured food. No talk, no recognition, no sharing, just the sound of one man frantically eating. This continued until dark. No stretching. No washing. No evening prayers. As if on cue, the Fatman simply fell asleep at the table, and, in less than ten minutes, began to snore. His guest began to doubt if he had knocked at the right door. Nevertheless, he decided to wait, say his prayers and practice patience. Luckily, the Besht was both hard of hearing and used to sleeping sitting up.

Next day was no different. By nightfall, he could take no more, felt ill and rose to leave. The Fatman, still wordless, waved farewell from his table.

"Before I go, sir," said the Besht, "allow me to ask you just one question. Why do you eat so much?"

"About time you asked," responded the host. He continued, "Because of my beloved father, blessed be his name. He was a thin, tiny man. When I was nine, we were walking in the snow-covered forests and were accosted by some Cossack soldiers.

They were drunk. They ordered my father to kiss the cross on the handle of a sword. He refused. [Deep breath]. They, they simply set him on fire, his beard first, and my father burned to death. Yes. In front of my two eyes. So fast. Two minutes . . . ashes in the snow. They laughed and let me go. I vowed that night never ever to die so fast, so helplessly. And so, my holy friend, I eat and I eat. This way, when they come for me, I will not disappear as did my father. Two minutes? No, I will be large, so large that" . . . as Wiesel tells it, "I would show them that a Jew does not go out like a miserable skinny candle . . . that is why . . all my passion is devoted to eating. Not that I am hungry, you understand. . . . . ." (*Souls on Fire* 27).

> One tradition of blasting the shofar during the High Holiday prayer is to penetrate the protective curtain of Heaven, thus forcing God to listen.

The story has an alternative ending. Sisyphus may indeed have his mountain, boulder and muscles with which to defy fate; the Fatman had only his weight, and it was enough. In Version II, the Fatman explains: "I will be so large, so fat that even the smoke rising from my corpse will not simply 'poof,' disappear. No, it will ascend, ascend all the way to Heaven. That way, God can no longer deny. He will have to look down at last and observe what truly transpires—the hatred and fury his creatures suffer only to sanctify His name." After a long silence, the Besht whispered, "I wish you a good Sabbath," then turned and, rather slowly, walked back to the edge of the forest.

Protests honed to an exquisite art—performed by Madmen. Vintage Wiesel.

Some may protest the sobriquet "madmen." How "mad" is it after all to give one's life in the heroic quest of awakening the conscience of one's assumed maker? For believers, the quest can be both heroic, since the Maker is at least possibly real, and futile—only if the Maker refuses to respond in an intelligible way or not at all. For those among us attracted by the clean, theology-free, bare-bones beauty and drama of the Sisyphus legend, the Fatman tale should end with "so I will not disappear in two minutes as did my father. . . ." Forget the superfluous, accusatory smoke rising upward. Keep the sky a God-free zone. The story's power remains intact. Many are those inclined to more fat on the bones and more mystery in the sky, drama rich in human complexity and messy contradictions inherent in common experience (let alone uncommon tragedy). For them, that essential smoke, directed to a real or imaginary God, must rise. Wiesel addressed this issue tangentially at a Holocaust conference where both he and a colleague, Rabbi Richard Rubenstein, were featured speakers. Rubenstein had just completed his lecture on post-Holocaust faith in which he outlined the existential trauma of and rationale for remaining a Jew in a Godless universe.

> **The pains of doubt did not end in faith. I eked my way toward allegiance first.**
>
> **HERBERT GOLD**

In the middle of Wiesel's extemporaneous response, referring to Rubenstein's admiring description of camp prisoners who secretly derived strength from their belief in God, Wiesel said, "And here I will tell you, Dick, that you don't understand *them* when you say it is more difficult to live today in a world without God. No! If you want difficulties, choose to live *with* God. Can you compare today the tragedy of the believer to that of the non-believer? The real tragedy, the real drama, is the drama of the believer" (Roth and Berenbaum 367).

That drama was unforgettably captured by the previously quoted hanging scene in *Night.* For a portrait of the believer in crisis one need only turn to the two Wiesel quotations from that scene chosen by the French author and Christian theologian, François Mauriac for his own introduction to Wiesel's testimony.

> "Never shall I forget that night,
> the first night in camp, which had
> turned my life into one long night,
> seven times cursed and seven
> times sealed. Never shall I forget
> that smoke. Never shall I forget
> the little faces of the children,
> whose bodies I saw turned into
> wreaths of smoke beneath a silent
> blue sky. Never shall I forget

those flames which consumed my
Faith forever. Never shall I forget
that nocturnal silence which
deprived me, for all eternity of the
desire to live. Never shall I forget
those moments which murdered
my God and my soul and turned
my dreams to dust. Never shall I
forget these things, even if I am
condemned to live as long as God
Himself. Never."

This identical passage is referred to by the Wiesel scholar Dr.
Joseph Lowin in his belief "that one day that's going to become
part of Jewish liturgy" (Lowin 6).

Mauriac's second example was the young Wiesel's reaction to
observing fellow prisoners cry a New Year's prayer.

"That day, I had ceased to plead,
I was no longer capable of
lamentation. On the contrary, I
felt very strong. I was the accuser,
and God the accused. My eyes
were open and I was alone—
terribly alone in a world without
God and without man. Without
love or mercy. I had ceased to be
anything but ashes, yet I felt

myself to be stronger than the Almighty, to whom my life had been tied for so long. I stood amid that praying congregation, observing it like a stranger." (*NIGHT* xx–xxi).

# Wounded Faith

THE FOLLOWING 5 QUOTATIONS, rich in their own ways, belong together and speak for themselves. The first two are taken from *ALL RIVERS RUN TO THE SEA,* written some thirty-five years after *NIGHT*.

> Sometimes we must accept the pain of faith so as not to lose it. And if that makes the tragedy of the believer more devastating than that of the non-believer, so be it (*Rivers* 84).

> I have never renounced my faith in God. I have risen against His justice, protested His silence and sometimes His absence, but my anger rises up within faith and not outside it (*Rivers* 84).

> Jewish tradition allows man to say anything to God, provided it be on behalf of man. Man's inner liberation is God's justification. It all depends on where the rebel chooses to stand. From inside his community, he may say everything. Let him step out of it, and he will be denied this right. The revolt of the believer is not that of the renegade; the two do not speak in the name of the same anguish (*Souls on Fire* 111).

**One can savor the juice of a fruit even as one throws away its peel.**

**REB MEIER**
**(Sea 364)**

19

In a video-taped interview with the religion correspondent for the *New York Times*, Wiesel was asked about this claim in his Nobel Peace Prize speech: "Action is impossible without faith." He replied:

> Once we realized the world turned against us we had all the reasons in the world to give up faith—but we didn't. I would lie to you if I told you that my faith today is the same as it was before the war. It is a wounded faith. . . . The Chassidic Master, Nachman of Bratzlav, said, "No heart is as whole as a broken heart." And that goes for faith as well. No faith is as whole as a broken, wounded faith. My faith is a wounded faith, but nevertheless, it's there . . . But I don't know what else to do" (WFPL Louisville, KY NPR station 2000).
>
> We must pass through a period of anguish and then a period of respite in order that in the end we may find or regain the faith of our Masters.
>
> Because without faith, we could not survive. Without faith, our world would be empty" (Dubois 67).

It's safe to speculate that these last two sentences would not sit well with Secular Humanists and perhaps seem irrelevant even to the Just Man of Sodom, the Fatman of the Forest and most certainly, Sisyphus, the Muscle Man of the Mountains. To use Wiesel's word, although a total loss of faith is certainly "understandable," for him, as we will see again and again, it is not an option.

To that, we must add one more "non-option." In *The 6 Days of Destruction* Wiesel states it thus: "The opposite of faith is not arrogance but indifference" (8). Indifference: the word perhaps most antithetical to his own nature. For that matter, antithetical, he argues, also to the nature of God. In Michael de Saint Cheron's book of interviews with Wiesel (*Evil and Exile*), the question arises of

> **Both the whole [Sinai] tablets and the shattered tablets lie in the holy Ark.**
>
> BABYLONIAN TALMUD
> Tractate Baba Bathra 14b

not man's but God's indifference. Wiesel responds: "Deep down, I feel a certain—and this is a Jewish certitude drawn from the sources of tradition—that an indifferent God is incomprehensible and inconceivable. An unjust God, yes. . . But an indifferent God is impossible" (Cheron 19). And if man's indifference (rather than arrogance) is indeed the true opposite of faith, what then the value, if any, of arrogance? "Occasionally useful," he might suggest. As for "ambivalence"? Inevitable. "Wounded Faith?" A tentative call for some measure of healing if possible, and only, if begun at all, gradually. "Was I later reconciled to Him? Let us say I was reconciled to some of His interpreters and to some of my prayers" (Rivers 84).*

---

* Readers familiar with the legendary dynamics of an abused son estranged from an absent, neglectful, or punishing father and their eventual hesitant reconciliation may find the depiction of God as an unjust yet eternally sought Father . . . especially intriguing.

# Mending Faith: Stage I

## God's Tears and Prison

A s a master of six languages, Wiesel is even more deeply enamored of silence. He writes rhapsodically of silence, its intoxicating freedom from the anguish of being misunderstood, of falling short of conveying the horrors and truths that reside well beyond the limitations of language. Profound as this reverence may be, it is no deeper than his hunger for music and the evocative powers of melody. Case in point: *Ani Maamin*. It is a song from his childhood, once sung at home, school and holidays in Sighet. The words *"Ani Maamin"* ["I Believe"] introduce an ancient declaration of faith in the eventual arrival of a Messiah. After the Death Camp liberation in his teens and the ensuing long silence, the melody was lost. Decades later, at a Passover meal, he heard it again, and the song became the title of his only cantata: *Ani Maamin, A Song Lost and Found Again*, score by Darius Milhaud (Sea 67). Concerning his attachment to the song itself, he explains:

Later I learned that Jews on their way to Treblinka and Birkenau had sung that song, as if to defy death. And I failed to understand: How could they believe in the coming of the Messiah *over there?* From where did they draw their faith in divine kindness and grace?

Then I sometimes question the child within me: What in the world was the Good Lord doing while His people were being massacred and incinerated?. . . Is it possible that in the midst of hell the victims kept their faith in a better world? Some witnesses answer affirmatively; I have no right to contradict them . . .

But then which approach is more justified? Both are, equally. There were Jews who prayed for the Messiah, and others who were ready to send him away. There were those who clung to the belief that all was not lost, and others who proclaimed that humanity was doomed. To say, as I do in my cantata, that the silence of God is God, is both an admission of resignation and an affirmation of hope.

The whole question of faith in God, surely in spite of man and perhaps in spite of God, permeates this cantata (Sea 68).

It is a question that must be asked again if the possibility of "mending" faith is ever to occur, and yet the cantata's answer, such as it is, remains, for some, stubbornly ambiguous. In the performance, Abraham, Isaac and Jacob may have the same problem. Their mission is to survey the Death Camps and report findings back to God. His eventual response? Tears and gratitude for the faith of

> For nothing can be sole or whole that has not been rent.
>
> CRAZY JANE
> by Yeats

His people, especially those *in extremis,* the very moment of their execution. Michael Berenbaum, referring to the cantata, in his study: *Elie Wiesel, God, The Holocaust and Children of Israel,* cautions, yes, "God too weeps even though He does not act and even though His tears are hidden from humanity" (111).

One wonders what the audience at Carnegie Hall on opening night, November 13, 1973, made of this chorus:

> *Ani maamin,* Abraham,
> Despite Treblinka.
> *Ani maamin,* Isaac,
> Because of Belsen.
> *Ani maamin,* Jacob,
> Because and in spite of Majdanek.

"Because" of Majdanek, the Jewish people must maintain their faith for without it they will disappear, leaving no one to bear witness? Is the song itself in danger of being lost yet again?" Or does "I believe '. . . Because and in spite of Majdanek'" imply an act of revolt against the forces of death and a silent God? The two young authors of *Hope Against Hope* ask Wiesel directly:

*B-K:* In the cantata, "I Believe" [*Ani maamin*] you write:
Despite Treblinka. I believe. Because of Belsen. I believe. Because of and despite Majdanek. I believe.

*EW:* This is a paradox. I deliberately use paradoxical language when it comes to the question of faith after the event. Wherever we turn after Auschwitz we find only despair. If we turn to God we ask ourselves: "How and why can I believe?" If we turn away from God we ask ourselves:"Where can I go?" To human beings? Have human beings earned our trust? And God? No matter in which direction we look we are surrounded by the same dark mystery. And the paradox in this is that despite everything and in defiance of everything we must have faith. Even if we find no faith we must raise it up in the hope that one day we will understand why, and that one day we will be able to give a reason for believing (Boschert-Kimmig 95).

The last two sentences of his reply deserve closer attention. After Auschwitz—a plea for hope, courage, faith, survival. Wiesel does not duck the apparent absurdity of this paradox. He declares it, embraces it "in defiance of everything," even in face of "the dark mystery" and chooses not to lose *Ani Maamin* again. Wiesel well understands how many survivors are legitimately drawn to a different conclusion than "one day we will understand." In fact, at the end of Stage IV in this study he will state: "And were God Himself to offer me an answer, any answer, I think I would reject it. For Treblinka has killed all answers." This is then followed in the ensuing section with a confession that, in his case, the very choice for faith is no authentic choice at all. For him to abandon faith, he claims, would require his transformation into another person. Another person, we might add, not deeply concerned with the quality of God's tears.

## God's Tears

Having declared allegiance to the camp of the faithful (though wounded), the ambiguities multiply. How is one now to respond to this "dark mystery" God? With indignation? With sadness? Consider these words from *All Rivers Lead To The Sea* . . ." Perhaps, God shed more tears in the time of Treblinka, Majdanek and Auschwitz, and one may therefore invoke His name not only with indignation, but also with sadness and compassion" (62). Yes, "compassion." Apparently the same compassion elicited by that child in *Night* gasping on the gallows. ("Where is God?" "He is hanging here on this gallows.") Indignation, sadness and compassion. And if compassion, how deep must it be to begin "mending" the wound? In his essay "The Solitude of God," Wiesel pursues the metaphor of divine tears:

> Naturally, like everyone else, I have known what it is to be angry and I have raised my voice in protest. I don't regret it. But with the passing of the years, I have come to understand. . . . He also has the right to ask us, "Why did you spoil my creation?" . . . Suddenly you think of God in His luminous, heavenly solitude, and you begin to cry. You cry for Him and over Him. You cry so much that He, too, according to Talmudic tradition, begins to cry, so that your tears and His tears meet and join together, as only two melancholy solitudes, thirsting for presence, may join together (reprinted in *Between Memory and Hope*, ed. Carol Rittner, p.7).

There may be something in the chemistry of black ink that, when mixed with the salt of tears, causes black prose to appear purple in the eyes of some readers. Purple or black, the image from Talmudic tradition of dual tears is a poignant reminder that God too allegedly has been "crying" with His people, and alone, for catastrophes long before our own. In ink that remains true black, Wiesel claims in *All Rivers Run to the Sea* that, as with the analogy of tears, "It is up to us to modify reality and make the prayer come true." Possible translation: if necessary, belief must "modify" (i.e., trump) reality. This rather startling admission may allow modifying our perception of reality (as in imagining that God metaphorically cries) so as to appear that prayers "come true" (God still feels for and loves us.). Admittedly, there is danger in such license since facile rationalization becomes a constant temptation. However, for one well grounded in religious tradition and wary of such pitfalls, there may also be opportunity for cogent insight, a boldness of vision that proves useful, even salutary and thus worth the reductionist risk. From a Wieselian perspective, the alternative, that reality, free of God and intrinsic meaning, be allowed to trump belief, remains totally unacceptable. Still no Sisyphus on Sinai.

In the ongoing attempts, over centuries, to fathom God's failure to surmount His tears and to act decisively in empowering His victimized children, Wiesel occasionally quotes one of his favorite sources, the Rebbe of Kotz, who "modified" man's helplessness by affirming: "I shall continue to call you Father until you become our Father." (Menachem Mendl of Kotz (1787–1859). If by virtue of such modifications we are better able to appreciate God's metaphoric tears, or His still emerging Fatherhood, so too will it help us visualize Master Kalman's allegorical elaboration of the image in his intriguing announcement of "the best-guarded secret since creation." The scene from *The Town Beyond the Wall* is a prison cell where the hero, Michael, is hallucinating an encounter with the wise elder, Master Kalman. "Master, I finally want to know God. I want to drag Him from His hiding place."

After brief exchanges, Kalman declares, "Yes, God is imprisoned. Man must free Him. That is the best-guarded secret since the creation" (10).

To which Reb Mendl might add: "free Him by calling Him Father." and Wiesel might rephrase as "giving back to God his own image" (*THE ACCIDENT* 42).

## Prison

Even extravagant characters in Wiesel's novels do not use the phrase "best-guarded secret in creation" lightly. Was that prison door locked before, during or after the Holocaust? If before or during, Master Kalman has provided God the prisoner with an ideal alibi for inaction. Or did he? If not the "prison" of Divine helplessness and tears (hence our compassion), consider the "prison" of indifference to gas chambers (hence our indignation and despair). It soon becomes arbitrary and thus unwarranted to push the compelling allegory of prison and escape much further. Indeed we have recently seen Wiesel reject the likelihood of an "indifferent" God as incompatible with Jewish tradition and with his own beliefs. Nevertheless, the possibility of Divine indifference does not leave quietly, and even as a whisper, in regard to gas chambers, the judgment may be too kind. The Chassidic Rebbe in *The Gates of the Forest*, whom we will again encounter shortly, abandons all restraint when he dares claim that which would justify a prison sentence of eternity since God "has become the ally of evil, of death, of murder" (196).

The anthropomorphic charges against and descriptions of God mount: sorrowful, helpless, indifferent, imprisoned, sadistic, allied with evil, emerging, fatherly. . . . Even some of these may not be the exact causes for imprisonment that Master Kalman has in mind with his "best guarded secret." He reveals only that God's freedom depends on man. This is not the same sermon message we have heard so often that God requires man's partnership as a co-creator in repairing the world. The "secret," much more intriguing, is that God needs man to open the prison door and allow/help God to be God. The strategy for escape—to do for God that which He cannot do for Himself—requires both compassion and a most stubborn and self-sacrificing devotion.

We are not talking here of only ritual observances, studies and prayers. In fact, Reb Mendl of Kotz, for one, is quite clear on the subject as Wiesel quotes him in *Souls on Fire*: "Who ever told you God is interested in your studies and prayers? What if He prefers your tears and suffering?"(235). And if so, is there any way that very suffering might be instrumental in unlocking God's allegorical prison door? Professor Byron Sherwin thinks so.

In his essay, "Elie Wiesel and Jewish Theology" (reprinted in *Responses to Elie Wiesel*, ed. Harry Cargas), Professor Sherwin offers this ancient key. "The meaning of suffering is its ability to elevate man above God, to secure His redemption from confinement. Suffering and evil are inherent in the process of redemption as well as of creation" (Sherwin 143). In a footnote, Sherwin claims, [Wiesel's] "theme of suffering and redemption . . . is quite complex and is expanded in his *The Beggars of Jerusalem*" (Sherwin 149). I must leave the untangling of that mystical complexity to others. Suffice this admonition on the value of suffering in Wiesel's response to a related question from his interviewer, Michael Cheron:

> The answer lies in the Jewish tradition, which denies the value of suffering. We do not believe that suffering can create or engender anything that transcends it. Suffering is not something one chooses. It is a persistent mystery, and we therefore try to make

something of it. But, I repeat, it would be against tradition to choose suffering" (Cheron 24).

In addition to the disturbing notion of Reb Mendl's "tears and suffering" as God's preference, as perhaps His ransom from prison, the quest for understanding variations of radical devotion must lead back to the railroad tracks and the root issue of man's tears and suffering, not for but due to God's alleged complicity (innocent or intentional, prisoner or not) in evil. It is best served by following the path to *A Journey of Faith* and Wiesel's startling response to a related question from Father John O'Connor.

## God's Guilt

Wiesel: Where is God? You ask? God is in prison. He is everywhere. If God is everywhere, he's also in everyone. In every act. And in every thought, in every tear, in every joy. And in evil. It's up to us to redeem that evil. But if I say God is not everywhere, God is not God. (O'Connor 8)

> **What?**
> **Shall we receive**
> **good at the hand of**
> **God and shall we not**
> **receive evil?**
> JOB, 11:10

We must go to *The Gates of the Forest* for amplification of this brazen notion. The Chassidic Rebbe here completes the speech from which a few words were quoted earlier. The subject, of course, is God.

He's guilty; do you think I don't know it? That I have no eyes to see, no ears to hear? That my heart doesn't revolt? . . . He has become the ally of evil, of death, of murder, but the problem is still not solved. I ask you a question and dare you answer: What is there left for us to do? (196)

Both Byron Sherwin and Michael Berenbaum, in separate studies, refer to this remarkable outburst as well as to Kalman's claim of God's imprisonment.

"What is there left for us to do?" Indeed. A familiar quandary. We have seen Wiesel ask himself in almost identical words the same question in the "Wounded Faith" section taken from his video interview. Significantly,

> If you are not my God, whose God are You? The God of the murderers?
>
> ZVI KOLITZ
> Yossel Rakover
> Speaks to God

he does not offer the standard Hebrew prayer for encountering evil (or for hearing of a death): "Blessed are You who are the true judge," meaning Who dispenses His judgments in a "true" way though beyond our understanding. Prayer or not, apparently, the one thing that is *not* "left for us to do" is abandon God in return. We have referred to this alternative as Wiesel's "non-option." So it is. So it remains at any cost. What distinguishes Wiesel from most others caught in this "drama of the believers" is the ruthlessness with which he faces these costs. The temptation of post-Holocaust faith can challenge one's intellectual honesty, integrity, harmony between head and heart, ability to recognize self-deception and, for some, challenge even one's sanity. Wiesel goes to the edge. And then some. . . .

## Holy Madness

Is God complicit with evil?

A guilty prisoner?

A helpless prisoner?

Weeping with His burning children?

On the gallows?

An intentional betrayer of the covenant?

A victim of Divine Madness?

Trapped between the silent skies of Auschwitz and his own refusal and inability to abandon faith, it's perhaps no wonder Wiesel began to question his own sanity. But not too fast: with Wiesel there is "insanity" and then there is "madness."

**Much Madness Is Divinest Sense.**
EMILY DICKINSON

In the book-length conversation with Harry Cargas, Wiesel admits his fear of insanity. "In order to save myself from *that* madness, I go back to another madness-a holy madness . . . the one that kept us alive for . . . thousands of years . . . No, I wouldn't say that I am not mad" (*Conversation* 2). The madness is holy because it cries to God and mad, of course, because the cry persists in spite of God's silence. Here is Michael speaking to Pedro in *The Town Beyond the Wall*:

Since the beginning of history, madmen have represented the divine presence: the light in their eyes comes bathed in the source . . . The choice of madness is an act of courage . . . It's an end in itself. An act of the free will that destroys freedom. Freedom is given only to man. God is not free . . . God too is trying to drive me mad"(94).

Michael's claim that madness is a "choice" disqualifies him from membership among the certifiably mad. His outbursts, though disjointed, are not insane nor necessarily shared by the author. There is no disagreement, however, that both holy madness and clinical insanity involve a fundamental break with rationality. The crucial acceptance of this fissure informs, resonates in and underlies much of what follows. To protest continually against an absent God may not strictly be "madness" and yet a more "sane" approach might consider the enterprise willfully blind to its own folly. Likewise, to forge from the shards of despair, abandonment, contradiction and paradox an inviolate attachment to that God does require (as we will see in Stage III) something beyond rational discourse—something perhaps a bit holy, courageous, and what may appear to some more than "a bit mad."

Before addressing the question of madness, in his "Partisan Guide" entitled *Choices in Modern Jewish Thought*, the theologian and professor of Jewish Religious Thought at Hebrew Union College, Eugene Borowitz, approaches the issue of Wiesel's overall influence on post-Holocaust theology with praise: "The pivotal figure in the resulting intellectual work is Elie Wiesel, though his works on the Holocaust are mainly fiction" (190). Pivotal, yes. Systematically, philosophically central, less so. "For all the influence of Wiesel's work, the theological discussion of the Holocaust has not centered about it because its format is intentionally ambiguous" (193). The modifier "intentionally" is crucial. The searing clarity achievable perhaps through "madness" may also destroy the ability or will to see at all. Hence the sunglasses of intentional ambiguity (e.g., . . . "intelligent madness") Borowitz perceives in Wiesel.

> Again and again he suggests that a species of intelligent madness is the most appropriate response to the Holocaust. Were we capable of becoming appropriately deranged, we might see in what now appears to us as blackest night. Philosophers who seek to "explain" the Holocaust are engaged in a self-contradictory project. Madmen are more truthful witnesses to the insanity we lived through (191).

May they only survive their madness.

Tales of bargaining with God, so frequent in the *Bible* and Folklore (see Genesis 19 and 28:22), unite those issues of madness, vain protest, persistence, fury and often invite, among the inevitable questions: Which party after all is the mad one, man or God?

Wiesel tells the old story of a rabbi confronting the village fool on the day after Yom Kippur:

> "So, Mendel, your seat was empty at prayer yesterday. You maybe were sick?"

"No, Rabbi, I was in the forest."

"Doing what?"

"Talking to God."

"About?"

"About my mother dying young. And plagues. And floods. And earthquakes. And evil people who stay rich. And the good who stay poor. Then I confessed skipping prayers and swearing and hitting my son and eating pork. We made a deal: If He would forgive my minor sins I would forgive His great ones."

"Mendel, you are a madman and a fool."

"For talking straight to God?"

"No!" said the rabbi. "For letting him off too easy!"

The supposition of madness, holy and otherwise, is not necessarily confined, according to Wiesel, to the human race. (His first play was titled *Zalmen: or the Madness of God.*) Consider this accusation against one possessing a most "unholy" derangement laced with gleeful sadism. It is hurled at the Almighty, Himself.

A few years later, I saw just pious men walking to their death, singing, "We are going to break with our fire, the chains of the Messiah in exile." That's when the symbolic implication of what my teacher had said struck me. Yes, God needs man. Condemned to eternal solitude, He made man only to use him as a toy, to amuse Himself. That's what philosophers and poets have refused to admit: in the beginning there was neither the Word nor Love, but laughter, the roaring, eternal laughter whose echoes are more deceitful than the mirages of the desert (*The Accident* 42).

Holy madness: exhibited, if not by the accused, then perhaps by the accuser. Although his name is Eliezer, a fictional survivor of the death camps and protagonist of Wiesel's novel, *The Accident*, the author assures us in the Preface: "I speak for my protagonist, but he does not speak for me. . ."

The protagonist of *The Town Beyond the Wall* (Michael quoted earlier on madness) is a survivor who returns to his hometown in Hungary after liberation, seeking his sanity and humanity. Arrested as a foreign agent, he befriends Menachim, a cellmate who helps him cry. It occurs after Michael saves Menachim from an attack from a hallucinating prisoner. They continually discuss God and madness until Menachim is transferred. Shortly before leaving, Menachim declares:" I prefer to be insane with God—or in Him—than without God or far from Him. . . . I prefer to blaspheme in God than far from Him" (165). If the laughing, cynical God imagined above from *The Accident* were somehow to hear of Menachim's poignant "preference" to "blaspheme in God" rather "than far from Him," it would likely be granted—with much amusement.

> **What's madness but nobility of soul at odds with circumstances?**
>
> ROETHKE
> "In A Dark Time"

# Mending Faith: Stage II

## Better to Blaspheme Than to Be Without God

THE POSTURE OF SIMULTANEOUS rejection of God as a source of compassion against dependence on Him for meaning and strength requires an agile mind with the balance of an acrobat. Pedro, Michael's dear friend in *The Town Beyond The Wall*, qualifies on both counts. Referred to as a "Madman's Prayer," here is his voice from that tightrope: "Oh, God, give me the strength to sin against you, to oppose your will! Give me the strength to deny you, reject you, imprison you, ridicule you!" (48). Talmud scholars are not the only ones who argue approvingly that paradox indeed goeth where mere rational discourse dare not tread. . . .

Moving from fiction to Wiesel's biography, we encounter three flesh-and-blood rabbis who were also camp prisoners with the author. In his introduction to *The Trial of God*, Wiesel explains: ". . . inside the kingdom of night, I witnessed a strange trial. Three rabbis, all erudite and pious men—decided one winter evening to indict God for allowing His children to be massacred. I remember: I was there, I felt like crying. But there, nobody cried." The play, inspired by the trial he witnessed, ends without a final verdict although it provides God with a brilliant defense attorney. We learn at the conclusion, His attorney was Satan.

In *Legends of Our Time*, Wiesel again returns to the challenge of religious observance in a camp dedicated to death. Our first encounter with the issue arose in *Night* where the teen-age Wiesel chose to ignore the required fast on Yom Kippur, the Day of Atonement. His cup of pale soup became his anti-prayer to his absent God (69). The drama intensifies in "Yom Kippur: The Day Without Forgiveness," as reported in *Legends*. Wiesel's friend and fellow prisoner, Pinhus, was once a director of a rabbinical school in Galicia. He now is feverish, near death, and tortured with the Wieselian quandary of observance versus rebellion on the holy day. How to express his indignation? As did his young friend, Wiesel? Not enough. Pinhus finally confesses that he indeed rebelled against God, not by eating on the holiest fast day of the year, but by fasting. "But not for the same reasons. Not out of obedience but out of defiance . . . here, it is by observing the fast that we can make our indignation heard. . . . Not for love of God but against God." He later asks Wiesel to say Kaddish for him.

> "But why?" I asked, "since you are no longer a believer?". . . .
>
> He replied: "Here and now, the only way to accuse Him is by praising Him."

Intentionally shaming God? Perhaps Pinhus' despair, inflamed by fever, finally unhinged his mind. Or, by way of obedient blasphemy, freed it. . . . Wiesel concludes the report: "and he went laughing to his death" (61).

To fast or not to fast is a problem that would not concern Michael of *The Town Beyond The Wall*, previously quoted. In her fine article, "Wiesel and the Absurd" (the last sentence of which is repeated in the Prologue) reprinted in *Responses to Elie Wiesel* (Harry Cargas, ed.) Josephine Knopp discusses now Michael's unique quandary where he cried:

> **The more you complain the longer God lets you live.**
> **JEWISH PROVERB**

> I want to blaspheme, and I can't manage it. I go up against Him, I shake my fist, I froth with rage, but it's still a way of telling Him that He's there, that He exists . . . that denial itself is an offering to His grandeur. The shout becomes a prayer in spite of me . . . (100).

Although Knopp does not argue that Michael necessarily speaks for Wiesel, she does claim Elijah in *Gates of the Forest* does so in his memorable:

> God's final victory, my son, lives in man's inability to reject Him. You think you're cursing Him, but your curse is praise: you think you're fighting Him, but all you do is open yourself to Him, You think you're crying out your hatred and rebellion, but all you're doing is telling Him how much you need His support and for-

giveness. No, you mustn't blaspheme against someone who shares your suffering . . . (42).

Elijah's first sentence presents the intriguing notion that man is ultimately incapable of rejecting God. He doesn't use the phrase "hardwired into our genes" as does the molecular biologist, Dean Hamer, in his book: *The God Gene: How Faith Is Hardwired into Our Genes*, but a brief meeting of minds is still possible—very brief. When Hamer declares, "My findings are agnostic on the existence of God" (TIME, 10-25-04, p 65), the meeting would end. He proposes that, as evolution favors strong societies over weak, faith accordingly tends to unite,

> Science gets better.
> Poetry doesn't.
> DEREK WALCOTT

humanize and overall strengthen those successful societies sufficiently and repeatedly until it becomes "hardwired" and thus passed on genetically. The so-called "God Gene" does its job in strengthening society into the "fittest" and thereby assuring its survival. The theory can be accepted by believers in their assuming God's signature to exist deep within our DNA as well as by agnostics who see only the grand, unfolding, hardwiring molecular biology of random mutation and natural selection.

The Elijah quote continues: "You think you're cursing Him, but your curse is praise. . . ." A curious footnote to some words of Job highlights the incidental connection between "curse" and "praise." Job said: "It may be that my sons have sinned, and blasphemed God in their hearts" (line 5). In explicating the phrase "blasphemed God," it's often been noted that "the Hebrew root usually means 'to bless'." Ibn Ezra points out that this is a euphemism for its opposite: "to curse, blaspheme." Rashi explains that out of motives of reverence, the verb "bless" was sometimes substituted for "curse."

If there are lines separating God-obsessions from God-intoxication, from God-addiction, they are lines many Wieselian characters (mad and not so mad) are prone to transgress. The turbulence and angst expressed in the preceding quotations just may, to the more mystically inclined, appear to be the fulfillment after all of Reb Mendl's declaration, quoted earlier, concerning God's possible preference for "suffering and tears" over study and prayer. However, if true to Jewish tradition, we need not doubt the likelihood that those opposed to the Rebbe's radical stance would find his words on suffering the most blasphemous of all.

# Mending Faith: Stage III

## Radical Devotion

"INSANITY" that can resonate as holy madness.

Blasphemy that becomes praise.

Praise that becomes accusation.

Abandonment that, as we shall see, begets not divorce but rebellion: a rebellion so radical that it transforms into an act of devotion. To witness in slower motion additional master strokes in this art of paradox, fury expressed not with fist but in the very joy of dancing, we must enter again the *Gates of the Forest* and first hear the uncanny Chassidic Rebbe explain:

> When you come to our celebrations, you'll see how we dance and sing and rejoice. There is joy as well as fury in the hasid's dancing. It's his way of proclaiming: You don't want me to dance: too bad, I'll dance anyhow. You've taken away every reason for singing, but I shall sing. . . . You didn't expect my joy, but here it is: yes, my joy will rise up: it will submerge you (196).

In *A Jew Today*, Wiesel, in his own voice, when asked about a God and a civilization that abandons its people replies with a similar paradox:

> **The road of excess leads to the Palace of Wisdom.**
>
> **BLAKE**

What must we do, what can we do in response? We must continue to sing. Because we have been hurt? No, more likely because we are mad. But ours is a different kind of madness: when the enemy is mad, he destroys; when the killer is mad, he kills. When we are mad, we sing (217).

"Could you explain the connection between joy and despair in Hasidism? Does joy lie within despair?" asks Michael de Saint Cheron in his series of interviews with Wiesel. The last two sentences of response: "But the great genius of Hasidism was that they found a joy within despair. Indeed, this is the purest joy of all, and the most noble."

Cheron, probably puzzled, persists: "Do you mean joy in spite of despair?"

Wiesel:

In spite of and within despair, for this joy does not deny despair. It is too powerful to be denied. But despite despair, within despair itself, there is a sort of space in which joy is both possible and necessary. Possible because necessary! That is the Hasidic joy. (Cheron 87)

Chassidic spirited singing and dancing as an expression of holy madness, joy, fury, protest, contradiction and, if you will, radical devotion, becomes a heady brew. One clean-shaven and marginal Jew not known for his singing or dancing (but a particular favorite of Wiesel) offers this from his novel *The Trial*: "The right perception of any matter and a misunderstanding of the same matter do not wholly exclude each other" (Kafka). Especially, may we add, when the "matter" involves rebellion through religious ecstasy.

> **When sorrow carves deeply into our hearts, it creates more room for eventual joy.**
> **PERSIAN PROVERB**

## Paradox

It is no secret that students of Talmud, let alone Kabbalists, like Wiesel, are drawn to paradox as a way of surmounting the "limitations" of linear, logical discourse. In a speech entitled "The Meaning of Freedom," Wiesel asks: "Does it seem like a paradox? I am free not to be afraid of paradoxes." A rare understatement. And why might one be "afraid of paradoxes"? Because of the contradiction at their heart that grins defiantly at our vain attempts to make "rational sense" of some non-rational experience. Blind faith for one. Referring to his cantata, Wiesel comments, "I deliberately use paradoxical language when it comes to the questions of faith after the event [of Auschwitz]." His ability not only to tolerate but to be comfortable with paradox and the contradictions thus implied is—for some, admirable, for others, disconcerting, and for most, noteworthy. Examples abound.

Among the nearly two dozen television interviews with Wiesel conducted by professor, author and editor, Richard D. Heffner, and collected in his *Conversations with Elie Wiesel,* one can find this response: "Yes, Richard, I'm not against contradictions. You know that. I'm not against contradictions; life is a contradiction. But what I would not like to have is a contradiction that turns against our fellow human brothers, companions, sojourners. The moment a contradiction turns against humanity, I discard it" (Heffner 156). Wiesel's essay "Shadows of Auschwitz" contains this confession: "If I told you I believe in God, I would be lying. If I told you I did not believe in God, I would be lying. If I told you I believed in man, I would be lying. If I told you I did not believe in man, I would be lying. But one thing I do know: the Messiah has not come yet" (Kolatch 248)

> I was of three minds,
> Like a tree In which
> there are three
> blackbirds.
>
> WALLACE STEVENS

For a Kabbalist, it is possible for God to be a helpless prisoner and yet omnipotent at the same time. Paradox allows one to oppose and condemn God by way of praising Him. It also can result in the "irrational" (but powerful) notion of admitting all the reasons in the world to deny one's Judaism and then myste-

> Do I contradict
> myself? Very well
> then, I contradict
> myself. (I am large. I
> contain multitudes.)
>
> WHITMAN

riously use the force of that very denial to embrace it. The first Prologue quotation to this monograph is a good example. We examine it shortly.

For now, suffice that Sisyphus, he who discovers in eternal slave labor both freedom and joy, as avatar for paradox and the Absurd, most likely would understand. If not, try tangentially the visionaries of modern science who also wrestle with complex paradox of a different order in their cosmic as well as subatomic research. Likely non-Kabbalists themselves, nevertheless in order to conceive of a boundless space that bends and time that ends, they too must conceptually transcend our more rational, Newtonian world.

> When logics die
> The secret of the soil grows through the eye
> And blood jumps in the sun.
> **DYLAN THOMAS**

## Facing Divorce

Though paradox may open some gates on the path to radical devotion, it is of questionable help in plumbing devotion's depth. Is there no wound deep enough to destroy Wiesel's faith? Apparently not. It is bottomless, invincible, and thus can withstand even the ultimate challenge—ordered directly from God Himself. Forget mere abandonment.

> Would that they had forgotten My name and done that which I commanded them.
> **TALMUD**

Imagine God demanding total divorce from His people. An end to Judaism. In a 1967 symposium, Wiesel states: "[If] You, God, do not want me to be Jewish: well, Jewish we shall be, neverthe-less, in spite of Your will" (*Judaism*, Summer, 67).

Jewish with or without God's will, that is,

but never Jewish without belief.

Later, in the same symposium, Wiesel makes clear his familiar refrain that belief does not require agreement. "The Jew in my view may rise against God, provided he remains within God. One can be a very good Jew . . . and yet be against God." And should this rejection of an imagined divorce decree from God occasion even greater punish-ment, consider this from the cantata *Ani Maamin*: "I believe in You/ Even against Your will/ Even if You punish me/ For believ-ing in You." These words, though written by Wiesel, are sung to God by a Patriarch from a depth of loyalty that borders on and then deepens into devotion. A devotion that survives apparently independent of the words, actions or inactions of the very Recip-ient of such worship.

We now turn to fifteenth-century Spain for a possible "ances-tor" of our singing, dancing Rebbe of protest. With a significant difference. No delirious dancing. No singing. No ecstasy. Instead, a clear, unequivocal declaration of belief. Within that belief: pro-found protest and rebellion—in words that nevertheless honor and worship God. Quintessential Wiesel. The speaker, recently expelled from Spain, has, in the last two days, buried his wife and two sons. We leave the world of fiction.

"Master of the Universe, I know what You want—I understand what You are doing. You want despair to overwhelm me. You want me to cease believing in You, to cease praying to You, to cease invoking Your name to glorify and sanctify it. Well, I tell you: No, no—a thousand times no! You shall not succeed! In spite of me and in spite of You, I shall shout the Kaddish, which is a song of faith, for You and against You. This song You shall not still. God of Israel."

**Mere Zeinen Doh!
(We are here!)**
SONG OF WARSAW
GHETTO UPRISING

And God allowed him to rise and go, farther and farther, carrying his solitude under a deserted sky (*A Jew Today* 164).

We do know this man. One possible descendent already identified is the Chassidic Rebbe of *The Gates of the Forest*, whose dancing is also fueled with fury and refusal to obey God's assumed wish for an end of celebration or of belief itself. (The fictional Rebbe allegedly is loosely based on Wiesel's friendship with the now deceased Lubavitcher Rebbe Schneerson.) Another familiar relative: the camp prisoner who, before execution, requests a Kaddish from Wiesel because "the only way to accuse Him is to praise Him" (*Legends* 61). Or to sing to Him, as does the cantata voice: "Even if You punish me/ for believing in You. . . ." Finally, the five word mantra from the author himself: "In spite of Your will," he declares in opposition to God's improbable divorce decree. Wiesel, though unique, is certainly not alone.

Apparently, fortunately, there are many Jews who simply will not/cannot let go. No matter what man or God says or does not say, does or fails to do, their faith and devotion, though radical, remain bedrock. The Rebbe calls it joy as well as fury. To release the tail of the Celestial Lion thrashing wildly to be free must risk being eaten alive or, as some might fear, risk losing one's soul altogether. Should the molecular biologists currently seeking evidence in our DNA for a "God gene" meet with success, thus explaining this irrational commitment, the tantalizing questions will remain: developed through evolution only? Placed by God independent of evolution? Placed by God via evolution? And finally, as with an unhealthy gene, should it be neutralized? Meanwhile, from laboratory to mediation center, what prognosis on the divorce proceedings imagined from God to His people? Only one: For those of Wieselian predisposition, the resolution contains no surprise—divorce attorneys need not apply.

> "... even if you wish to, you cannot escape God's snares. You cannot cease to pray ..."
>
> AARON ZELTLIN

## The Man That I Am

The next quotation includes this intriguing phrase: "For me, *the man that I am* (my italics), . . . It is even possible for me to remain true to myself and be against God, but never without God." The unexpected emphasis on "man that I am" suggests a humble acceptance of one's own idiosyncratic strengths and limitations. It implies: **You, reader are not me. You are the man or woman _you_ are (divorce God- prone or not) and thus may require a different formulation of belief or disbelief. I can only speak for myself, limitations and all.** The phrase "man that I am" is repeated in a quotation at the end of this monograph which overlaps here with its relevant reminder from Job: "Even if He kills me, I shall continue to place my hope in Him." Menachem from _The Town Beyond the Wall_ could join this chorus with his "I prefer to be insane with God . . . than without God," thus certifying his Jobian credentials. Final consensus on divorce from at least our selected Wieselian ensemble: It remains "Till death do us part" . . . (if even then).

As the mere label "paradox" fails to help us unravel the mystery of its mystical attraction to the religious mind, so too does the adjective "radical" prove incapable of capturing the

> **The god of galaxies . . . how shall we praise Him? for so we must, or wither.**
> **MARK VAN DOREN**

resilience of such devotion when stretched almost to its absolute breaking point. Wiesel, now in his own voice, cools the modifier in a less incendiary interview with two students of Christian theology who otherwise would perhaps be unaccustomed to such audacious declarations of allegiance.

One of the most serious questions I have confronted over the years is whether one can still believe in God after Auschwitz. It

was not easy to keep faith. Nevertheless, I can say that, despite all
the difficulties and obstacles, I have never abandoned God. I had
tremendous problems with God, and still do. Therefore I protest
against God. Sometimes I bring God before the bench. Nevertheless, everything I do is done from within faith and not from out-
side. If one believes in God one can say anything to God. One
can be angry at God, one can praise God, one can demand things
of God. Above all, one can demand justice of God. As a Jew I
place myself within the tradition, the tradition of Moses, Jere-
miah, Job, and countless talmudic masters. Like me, they all had
difficulties with God. But God also has difficulties with me. I do
not think that what I am saying here about my being a Jew, Christians would say about being a Christian. For me, *the man that I
am* [my italics], it is possible to be for God with God. It is even
possible for me to remain true to myself and be against God, but
never without God (Boschert-Kimmig 91).

Parenthetically, the above phrase "never abandoned God" echoes the same verb used near the end of NIGHT in describing
Wiesel's temporary though traumatic neglect of his dying father:
"I had known that he was on the brink of death and yet I had
abandoned him. . . . Immediately I felt ashamed of myself,
ashamed forever" (*NIGHT 106*). Shame is not the issue in Stan-
ley Kunitz's great poem "Father and Son," since, if biographical,
the father took his life months before his abandoned son's birth.
An ocean away from Auschwitz and yet the son's lament is somehow appropriate: "Father!" I cried, "Return! You know the

way. . . . Instruct/ your son, whirling between two wars,/ In the Gemora of your gentleness . . . / O teach me how to work and keep me kind." Two qualities, no less, each writer possesses in abundance.

> In my soul I feel just that terrible pain of loss, Of God not wanting me— of God not being God— Of God not existing . . .
>
> —MOTHER TERESA

# Mending Faith: Stage IV

## "Nevertheless I Celebrate You"

IN 2002, WIESEL AGREED TO A VIDEO-TAPED "First Person Singular" self-interview, produced and directed by Robert Gardner, with selections of his work read by the actor William Hurt and funded by Boston University and a number of foundations. Of interest to our focus on "devotion" are his addresses to God in a voice resembling an angry parent and later a scorned partner again resisting divorce. Referring to himself after liberation, around age 17:

> I became religious. Even more so. Maybe I also wanted to prove something to God. "You didn't behave well. Nevertheless, I shall behave well toward You. You owe me something. I owe You nothing. *Nevertheless I shall continue praying to you, and celebrating you"* [my italics] In spite of everything else, I never divorced God. Couldn't. I'm too Jewish. I came from too Jewish a background. My Jewish heart is too Jewish. Everything about

> Tevya spoke to his horse as though it were his God, and spoke to God as though He were his horse. Kierkegaard would never understand.
> **IRVING HOWE**

me is Jewish. But I said to myself: I do believe in God. But I have a right to protest against His ways. I have the right to be angry, and so I do it a lot. Very often. I wouldn't change a word . . . Because I came to a certain formulation: a Jew or a man can be religious or come from a religious background with God, against God, but not without God. So I cannot live without God.

Indeed, it would not be difficult to transpose some of Wiesel's monologue here and elsewhere to partners in a difficult love relationship that has seen better days. The fundamental commitment of at least one partner is unshakeable but that is no protection from the articulated feelings of disappointment, anger, recrimination, regret, confusion followed by resolution to try again. "Nevertheless." Previously noted: "and yet." Frequently quoted: "on the other hand" and "in spite of." All signature Wieselian expressions especially predictable on the root issue before us. Eventually, with patience and luck, the agitated air temporarily clears, providing opportunity for mending wounds and subdued celebration. Consider this New Year Greeting from Wiesel in the *New York Times*.

As we Jews now enter the High Holidays again, preparing ourselves to pray for a year of peace and happiness for our people and all people, let us make up, Master of the Universe. In spite of everything that happened? Yes, in spite. Let us make up: for the child in me, it is unbearable to be divorced from you so long (October 2, 1997).

## The Decisive Link

The focus can now shift from accusation to what Wiesel calls a "decisive link" and even a locus where he claims God can always be found. Appropriately, these revelations are discussed in the *Hope Against Hope* interview.

> **Love calls us to the things of this world.**
> **ST. AUGUSTINE**
> **quoted by Richard Wilbur**

Jewish tradition is that we human beings are responsible for one another. We are also responsible for God. Perhaps that sounds presumptuous, but it isn't. It is God's will that we are responsible for God's creation, for God's creatures, and for the creator Himself.

In our tradition we say that regarding the Messiah, it is not God who makes the decision. God does not decide when the Messiah comes; we do. When we change the world so that it is ready and worthy, then the Messiah will come. *I am convinced that this is the decisive link between human beings and their creator.* [my italics] (Boschert-Kimmig 92).

We do not know whether the Messiah is a personal Messiah, a particular person or a time; perhaps he is an epoch. This is all left intentionally in doubt. However, all those who believe in the different versions hold one thing in common: we all believe in waiting (Boschert-Kimmig 93).

The French writer and archivist, Michael de Saint Cheron (who in mid-life embraced Judaism) published his many interviews with Wiesel in his previously quoted *Evil and Exile.* On the issue of Messiah as decisive link, Cheron asks: "Do you ever find yourself thinking, as Kafka did, that the Messiah will come not on the last day but on the day after the last?" Wiesel responds:

> I love Kafka. There is such a power in everything he wrote! That is a magnificent phrase, sober and somber. Sometimes I think that we are condemned to wait without end, that we Jews live in suspension, that when the waiting is over, we will have to wait yet again, that even after the last day, there will be yet another day, the last of the last, the post-ultimate (Cheron 75).

> **Man is in love**
> **And loves what**
> **vanishes. What more**
> **is there to say?**
> YEATS
> *
> *
> *
> **(. . . plenty!**
> WIESEL)

And should that post-ultimate day ever arrive, Wiesel will not be the first in line. In his powerful essay, "To A Young Jew Today," found *in One Generation After*, he offers this warning: "Two thousand years of exile have taught [the Jew] to wait for the Messiah and to suspect him once he has arrived" (*Generation* 165).

Clearly, the period of waiting is not wasted in idle years of gazing skyward. Not with a world filled with sorrow and opportunities for love, often as close as across a backyard fence.

## Where God is to Be Found

*I am absolutely convinced that God is to be found in a simple human relationship* [my italics]. *We have few certainties, but this is*

*one of them. When two people love one another, God is there. God*
*is present when people are present to and for one another in a*
*human way. God does not say, "Your life belongs to me." God says,*
*"Your life belongs to your neighbor"* (Boschert-Kimmig 99).

To which a presumptuous Wieselian might add: feeling compassion for and loving one's neighbor coincidentally could also be
seen as yet another way of celebrating God.

Were the last two sentences of this quotation repeated out of context, and in the company of the Secular Humanists among us, they
might understandably consider Wiesel one of

> **If you hallow this
> life you meet the
> living God.**
> BUBER

their own. I too have wondered if he might ever slip out the back
door and cross that very street. Only "when night comes during
mid-day" (Yiddish expression). Translation: Never. Almost every
quotation in this rough "scrapbook" mitigates against such a
defection. When "your life belongs to your neighbor," the Wieselian implication indeed is that you thereby honor the holiness
of that neighbor, one source of which is God. Granted, the very
term "neighbor" is understood in its broadest (and Humanist)
definition. Winning the Nobel Peace Prize was due in part to
Wiesel's bearing witness to the plight of neighbors in Biafra, Par-
aguay, Vietnam, Ruwanda, Darfur to name a few. Caring for,
bearing witness, loving, celebrating fellow humans is a persistent
theme in his novels, often as a reaction, an antidote against
despair. Though therapeutically sound, the Jewish injunction of

"Repairing the World" in fact can also be understood as obedience to God's original intention that "Your life belongs [not to Him] but to your neighbor." And, for some (Wiesel among them), caring about and for one's neighbor is precisely one of the many places He can be found.

In a speech to the students of Queen's College, New York City, 1994, Wiesel pursues the "nexus of God in human relationships": "If I want to come closer to God . . . it is only by coming closer to my fellow human beings. . . . If I am your friend, I am God's friend. If not, I am the enemy of both God and his creatures" (Kolatch 73). However, it is usually the human relationships that he states first. Four years later, in the May 1998 issue of *Civilization*, he writes:

> . . . it is to the human being and almost for the human being that I cling desperately to God. If I were to give up on humanity, I think I would give up on God. But I am not giving up, and therefore I am not giving up on God, either (Kolatch 293).

Most Secular Humanists will meet him half way. They also do not give up on humanity, but do manage to express their compassion in a non-theistic vocabulary.

By tying his faith in God to his faith in humanity, Wiesel extends the original notion of celebrating God noted in the opening quotation of this Stage IV. Later, from that same "First Person Singular" self-interview, Wiesel elaborates even the concept of bearing witness to man and God by quoting God's words as stated in the Talmud: "If you are my witnesses, I am God: if you are not my witnesses, I am not God." If God needs our witness in order to be God, He may also require our rescue of Him in order to be our Father. Reb Mendl of Kotz said it well in our first encounter with "God's Tears." His variation on celebrating God through witness offers an intriguing notion that now bears repetition: Wiesel translates: "I shall continue to call You Father until You become our Father."

> It is not necessary to accept everything as true. One must only accept it as necessary.
>
> KAFKA

It occurs that bearing witness to man and to God, believing in a "decisive link between human beings and their creator," recognizing Him, in fact, finding Him in "simple human relationships," helping Him truly become "our Father" may indeed involve more than a Wieselian celebration of God. Would not a learned Kabbalist maintain that, as suggested, they also do serve as possible strategies to help release Him from that "best-guarded secret since creation," God's metaphorical prison? When so conceived, for the Kabbalist at least, the significance of Witnessing must increase profoundly. (The Secular Humanist Congregation finished their services hours ago. . . . ) Those of us less at home with the Kabbalist language of paradox and metaphysical supposition may content ourselves observing that, as demonstrated previously, some wounds to faith, with time and effort, may seem responsive to mending after all. To be more precise, one might seek a distinction between those wounds amenable to sutures and those which are still beyond the healing powers of time and diligence.

Here, at the end of "Mending Faith: Stage IV," we have considered many quotations, and yet, in truth, have never left "those wounds beyond healing," i.e., the hanging child scene in *Night* and its essentially unanswered original question: "Where is God?" More than a half century later, Wiesel is still asking, but now with a seasoned resolve: "He could have, He should have terminated the torment of the innocent. Why didn't He do it? I don't know and I think that I shall never know. Undoubtedly, He does not wish me to know." God has an answer, we ask, and withholds it? Out of pity? Cruelty? Indifference? Later in the same lecture ("The Solitude of God," Lecture at 92nd St. Y, October 31, 1985) he continues: "Nothing justifies Auschwitz, and were God Himself to offer me an answer, any answer, I think I would reject it. For Treblinka has killed all answers." This echoes an equally unequivocal and yet slightly modified declaration found in his letter "To a Young Jew of Today:" "If God is an answer, it must be the wrong answer. There is no answer" (*Generation* 166). But the questions never end. This response at the end of a lecture Wiesel delivered in 1995: "I am not at peace. I never said I lost my faith in God. I was angry. I still don't understand God's ways. If He was going to explain the Holocaust, I

would say no, I want the wound to remain open. And it is"
(Kolatch 205).

> Mending that doesn't mend.
> Healing that doesn't heal.

> *"The injury cannot be healed, it extends through time,*
> *And the Furies, in whose existence we are forced to*
> *Believe . . . perpetuate the tormentor's work by denying*
> *Peace to the tormented."*
>
> —PRIMO LEVI
> Epigraph to Stanley Kunitz's poem
> "In the Dark House"

---

**He lives below the
senseless stars
And writes his
meanings in them.**
**THOMAS WOLFE**

---

# God's Inner Circle

## Three Declarations

I HAVE SAVED THREE of Wiesel's unique confessions of faith for the end. The presumptuous heading of "God's Inner Circle" refers to an imaginary gathering of past and present holy men and women about to include various victims and survivors of the Holocaust. Prominent among them are those whose God-intoxicated devotion becomes radicalized in part by their refusal to compartmentalize Auschwitz. Instead, they live and speak and pray their desperate hunger for God simultaneously with their confusion and fury. Like Wiesel, they disregard what some may call common sense and simply will not let go of Him.

Like Wiesel, they are no longer soft-spoken. They know how to Pray. Somehow, with both eyes open. Indirectly referring to someone very like himself, Wiesel claims, "Even in heaven, in that world of truth, he will stand before the celestial throne and say, 'Look! Look at the flames that burn and burn, hear the mute cries of Your children as they turn to dust and ashes'" (*Rivers* 89). The members of this fictitious, exclusive circle would understand, all too well, the following three selections. They could all meet in a very small room.

## I. To Be a Jew

. . . But to be a Jew is to have all the reasons in the world to destroy and *not to destroy*! To be a Jew is to have all the reasons in the world to hate the Germans and *not to hate them*! To be a Jew is to have all the reasons in the world to mistrust the church and *not to hate it*!

TO BE A JEW IS TO HAVE ALL THE REASONS IN THE WORLD NOT TO HAVE FAITH IN LANGUAGE, IN SINGING, IN PRAYERS, AND IN GOD, *BUT TO GO ON TELLING THE TALE, TO GO ON CARRYING ON THE DIALOGUE, AND TO HAVE MY OWN SILENT PRAYERS AND QUARRELS WITH GOD* (Roth and Berenbaum 369) [italics and capitalization mine].

Some ignore the Absurd. Some deny it. Others (like Sisyphus) fight it. Wiesel somehow converts the inert matter of despair and sorrow into a highly charged and prophetic defiance that sustains and empowers him on the long journey back to his "silent prayers and quarrels with God." Yes, the last sentence (capitalized) already served as Prologue; fifty words packed as carefully as a prose poem. I find the honesty both bracing and beautiful.

> **"One has to be mad today to believe in God and in man . . . Be mad, Rabbi, be mad!"**
>
> ZALMEN
> Or the Madness of God

Tragic, yes. But in its boldness, its clear admission of "all the reasons in the world not to . . ." and yet its seemingly mad insistence on faith (however fractured) . . . the devotion becomes mysterious, perhaps Absurd and radical by its very achievement.

We have been trying, through four stages, to get over that middle word, "but." Before it is The Problem ("not to have faith"), and after it a response if not quite a Resolution (tales, dialogue, prayers, quarrels). "To be a Jew" according to the last sentence acknowledges the existence of powerful reasons not to have faith in (1) language, (2) singing, (3) prayers, (4) God. The ostensible implication because of and despite those very reasons is to transcend them by way of the same leap modeled above with the reversal "not to hate" Germans and "not to hate" the church. One then expects an exhortation to do so, to remedy the threat of lost faith in the same three activities and in God by transforming that loss as well into an equally rebellious counter-force of investing faith. Thus, out of at the very least a furious ("I'll show them") indignation, the implication would call for a YES, a restoration of faith in singing and in language. (A variation on "Living well is the best revenge.")

As for the expected YES also to prayers and to God, the same assumptions of defiant counterforce would apply. That is unless they do not apply at all. Notice the anticipated exhortation for a resumption of faith in any one of the four—language, song, prayer, God—in fact never arrives. This invites the alternate, more literal and assumption-free reading in which "to have all the reasons in the world not to have faith" simply describes those to whom the reasons are already sufficiently persuasive to indeed effect a partial or total abandonment of such faith. Consider Secular/Humanistic Judaism wherein the reflex of rebellion against Nazi attempts to destroy faith in language, song, prayer, God has restored faith, if at all, only to language and song. With its emphasis, among others, on Jewish cultural survival, references to prayers and a personal God are often replaced with an approximation of belief in "the selected wisdom of our forefathers and the realistic application of those values on one's personal life and on a suffering world." Significantly, be it religious faith, a resistance-based faith, lost faith, or faith that never was, the Wieselian commitment ("but to go on telling the tale . . .") becomes the one sure act of rebellion that is not merely assumed but declared as independent, intact and incumbent upon all Jews.

Should this more literal reading of Wiesel's words seem a bit narrow, so it is, but no less likely than an imagined call assumed through implication only—for a restoration of faith including prayer and God when no such call had been articulated. True Wieselians might respond that both alternatives—action based on faith including prayer and God, or on faith limited to language and song—are each genuine and valid. They might further suggest the Talmudic possibility that one alternative is merely whispered between the lines of the other. . . . Wiesel's personal response appears suddenly in the quotation's last ten words: "and [for me] to have my own silent prayers and quarrels with God." It breaks from the subject ("To be a Jew") in mid-sentence to introduce a final confession not necessarily intended for readership adoption ("have my own") and is composed in part of quarrels. Might not those quarrels also concern the crisis of faith?

Among those unwilling or unable to follow suit and venture their own prayers and quarrels with God, the reflexive (and for some counter-intuitive) six imperatives clearly still apply. They including learning to withhold revenge and destruction, to not hate Germans or the church, to reconsider faith in at least language and singing and unequivocally to tell the tale, carry on the dialogue. Together or in part, these Wieselian resolutions serve to honor, fortify and help define what it means today to be a Jew. However, should they in fact help or not help is somewhat beside the point. Are they not then also intended as lessons for mankind? Wiesel's public stance in opposition to hate and violence is at odds with his private fears as to the improbability that these convictions might actually influence national policies. Intention: Peace. Expectation: dubious at best. His words from a TV interview: "If Auschwitz didn't cure the world of Anti-Semitism, what will and what can?" (Charlie Rose, June 22, 2004). Nevertheless, as classic victims and rare survivors of the Art-Beyond-Comprehension of Genocide, the Jewish people inherit, if you will, the virtually "self-certifying" and for some, "sacred" mission of keeping alive their unbelievable tale from generation to generation. As for the above-mentioned help or no help in defining their Judaism? As for hope or no hope that the world will listen? Wieselians, I would venture, speak ultimately closer to the bone: Tell the tale. Because it happened. That's why.

> **"To my father, every grandchild that's born, it's like a jab to the Germans."**
>
> BEN ZION HOROWITZ
> in Chassidic documentary
> "A Life Apart"

Accordingly, he leaves his readers with a provocative, non-negotiable obligation to disseminate the World War II history of, among others, Jewish extermination and survival for as long as there are friendly and not friendly ears to hear, eyes to read and minds to respond. And when the current tellers and their words are gone? A reply transposed from the past about which he might not demur: To be a Jew, . . . "Thou shalt teach them diligently to thy children, speak of them when in thy house, when thou walkest by the way, when thou liest down, when thou risest up . . ." (Deut. 6:4). A renowned Holocaust scholar reminds us that should the teller be a Secular Jew or a Secular non-Jew, it follows that "a secular holiness, as it were, has forced itself into his/her vocabulary" (Fackenheim 86). Sisyphus would question "holiness" . . . but otherwise once again understand. The rest indeed is dialogue—and commentary.

"To go on telling the tale" for whatsoever reason, although not obvious at first, is also a universally understandable response. It is one way, everlastingly poignant, to honor the final wishes for permanent memory from those who died defiantly and not defiantly but, as some survivors have felt, in our place. "Poignant" in the sense only that should we remember or forget, the dead will never know. Consequently, one might argue, the privilege to remember falls even more urgently on those of honor who do follow. Remember and respond by way of memorials, museums, ceremony, courses, research, scholarship, symposia, literature, the arts and by telling the tale. Tell it with God and tell it without God and tell it always, according to Wiesel, with dialogue. *

Why dialogue? With whom? With only listeners to the tale? *For non-believers, yes.* Dialogues with God, too? For Wiesel, of course ("and to have my own"). For believers fraught with doubt or outrage? Although no one size nor one soul fits all, the following "Prayer" by Wiesel, intended for the wounded in faith, comes close. It models an approach for breaking the anguished silence of religious despair as long as "dialogue" is understood to entertain the possibility of but one voice speaking. Short of prayer, however, merely preserving the tale, encouraging the dialogue and God-centered questions it sometimes raises, may

> And we enter the dialogue of our lives that is beyond all understanding or conclusion. It is mystery. It is love of God. It is obedience.
> **MARY OLIVER**

---

* Strategies for generational memory preservation by way of personal and family ritual, as with the Passover Seder, are available in the writings of Rabbis Avi Weiss and Neil Gillman.

concomitantly aid those of troubled faith in their personal turns either toward or away from God.

Wiesel's turn here continues with "my own silent prayers" (which may include those that arise on their own) followed by the Wieselian trademark: "and quarrels with God." Apparently the quarrels follow prayers, are part of prayers, but are not the full substance of prayers. Finally, if dialogue is indeed with God, does that not imply two voices? These ambiguities, I maintain are yet further instances of what Professor Eugene Borowitz refers to as Wiesel's "intentional ambiguities" (Borowitz 193).

"But one can't get there from here."

He just did.

## II. Prayer

What follows is not a silent prayer and quarrel with God but rather a prayer made public, though in mood, not far from a quarrel. It merits careful reading:

### Prayer

[1]   I no longer ask You for either happiness or paradise; all I ask of You is to listen and let me be aware of Your listening.

[2]   I no longer ask You to resolve my questions, only to receive them and make them part of You.

[3]   I no longer ask You for either rest or wisdom, I only ask You not to close me to gratitude, be it of the most trivial kind, or to surprise and friendship. Love? Love is not Yours to give.

[4]   As for my enemies, I do not ask You to punish them or even to enlighten them; I only ask You not to lend them Your mask and Your powers. If You must relinquish one or the other, give them Your powers. But not Your countenance.

[5]   They are modest, my requests, and humble. I ask You what I might ask a stranger met by chance at twilight in a barren land.

[6]   I ask You, God of Abraham, Isaac and Jacob, to enable me to pronounce these words without betraying the child that transmitted them to me: God of Abraham, Isaac and Jacob, enable me to forgive You and enable the child I once was to forgive me too.

[7]   I no longer ask You for the life of that child, nor even for his faith. I only beg You to listen to him and act in such a way that You and I can listen to him together (*Generation* 189).

Twelve sentences into seven brief stanzas, the first five of which sound more like an anti-prayer. Instead of the more familiar praises to God and supplication for assistance and guidance, we find stanzas 1–3 each begin "I no longer ask You" followed by "I do not ask You" and "I only ask You not . . ." in stanza 4. "I no longer ask You" returns to begin the final stanza. If this were a more traditional prayer, especially in a Christian setting, one would expect reference to God as the source of divine love. Instead, we find in stanza three the startling: "Love, love is not Yours to give." Not a mere observation. Try accusation. Apparently, love, if available at all, must come from human relationships and human only. God missed His chance. Six million of them.

The bitterness continues almost to the edge of sarcasm in stanza 4. If You insist on aiding my enemies with "Your mask and Your powers," he bargains, and are willing or able to withhold only one, "give them Your powers. But not Your countenance." (Not Your mask, not Your favor.) These audacious instructions to a traditional God are immediately followed by the chastened claim that they are "modest" and "humble" (stanza 5), probably because they are neither. One can imagine the speaker shocking himself with his own boldness. His voice in stanzas 1–5 may seem quiet, even passive, ostensibly asking for so little, but the implications for an allegedly merciful and compassionate God are devastating. Stanza 5 ends with a landscape of estrangement ("stranger," "chance," "twilight," "barren land") so stark, attempts at even the most basic man/God communication would dissolve in futility.

Can this relationship be saved? Only with the help of a third party. A child. A child referred to six times in the last six lines. A child who does not inhabit that "barren land" but rather refers to God as still the "God of Abraham, Isaac and Jacob." The child of deep and innocent faith that Wiesel once was and still holds dear. With his appearance, the once passive voice becomes active. The "I no longer ask You" litany is now reversed with "I ask You" and a double request of "enable me" (stanza 6). The final stanza ends with the most traditionally prayerful and now active-voiced: "I only beg You to listen . . ."

The child is magic. The purity of his faith allows the adult he becomes to now twice identify God as "God of Abraham, Isaac and Jacob." William Wordsworth had it right: the child indeed "is father of the man." So much so that the father fears "betraying" the pre-war child that he was and longs for the child to forgive him. For what? Apparently for losing the intimacy with God he, as a child, once so profoundly possessed. To achieve this mystical self-forgiveness, the man needs God's help. But an even greater task awaits—he must first forgive God. And for this too he feels helpless and in need of divine assistance: ". . . enable me to forgive You and enable the child I was to forgive me too." Short of accomplishing this double request, the last line may never come to pass: "I only beg You to listen to him and act in such a way that You and I can listen to him together." Together. After forgiveness? Before forgiveness? With no forgiveness? Although the longed-for reunion of man, child and God is a distant goal, it is also thankfully a long way from that "barren land."

On first reading, the Prayer seems to move from a barely concealed angst and seething anger to sufficient reconciliation for the three of them—God, child and man—together to listen as the child of pure and uncorrupted faith speaks to his God and the man he will become. And then the second reading: we feel the tug of an undertow. Reconsider that last sentence: "I only beg You to listen . . . You and I can listen to him together." Yes, you "can," *if* that God of Abraham, Isaac and Jacob agrees to join you, agrees to listen to that child within you say his piece. . . . It may be a long wait. The likelihood of that trio actually meeting seems doubtful. After all, this prayer is a hopeless accumulation of "I no longer ask You," previously failed requests, ignored pleas, cries and supplications. No answers then. Perhaps no answers now.

We move to the third reading. Apparently God need do nothing about the requests of this prayer for them to appear satisfied. He is relieved from providing "happiness or paradise," relieved from resolving questions, relieved from providing "rest or wisdom," most defiantly relieved from providing love, relieved from punishing or enlightening the enemy, relieved even from providing the life or faith of the child who became the author of this Prayer. In essence, He need "provide" nothing. He need only refrain from taking away anything more. Especially memory of a holy childhood. How likely then that He join the speaker in listening to the child, enable the *double* forgiveness (stanza six), and let it be known that He listens? Will he keep His "Countenance" to Himself? For that matter, is He even listening? Is He there? And how will we ever know?

The last three questions are not Wiesel's. For others, they are hard to avoid. With God relieved of so many demonstrable responses initiated by prayers, the few remaining "modest" and "humble" requests could be "fulfilled" with no one actually at the wheel. Should the supplicant, through his own inner-work achieve some measure of self-forgiveness and feel an authentic or perhaps imagined spiritual closeness, he might in fact understand (or misunderstand) his prayers as answered. I indulge this sophistry only to highlight a fundamental strength of the work. It can be read as a cautious affirmation of faith and with equal justification as simply a way to frame and understand a solely natural cause and effect experience in a comforting and traditional but now quasi-religious vocabulary. What might seem to some a faulty ambivalence in the Prayer's basic structure (Can it go toward and away from God at the same time?) is in fact one source of its virtuosic power. It may also be an example of what Eugene Borowitz referred to in Stage I on Holy Madness as Wiesel's "intentional ambiguity."

We have seen briefly in his novels, by daring to probe such paradoxical contradictions woven into human experience, Wiesel strikes closer to the bifurcated truths of our lives. Scholars argue that even some Psalms lend themselves well to such multi-directional readings. ("To whom does the atheist give thanks?" asks the wise man. "Why, to the God in whom he no longer believes.") If this be mere playing with words, it is indeed as

Robert Frost maintains regarding his vocation, work that "is play for mortal stakes, . . . For heaven and the future's sakes."

The Prayer speaks to both the disillusioned believer and the non-believer who still needs to pray. (The non-believer with no need to pray will take his business elsewhere.) Its final judgment on faith occurs in the penultimate line, "I no longer ask you for the life of that child, nor even for his faith." Though fresh and beautiful, the child's faith remains naïve and necessarily blind to the consequences of on-rushing history. For many, only faith complicated and tested by wounds of doubt and abandonment possesses sufficient "authority" for relevance and meaning in a post-war world. As with this Prayer.

The ability to communicate conflicting ideas in a single expression is one of the glories and demons of our language. Consider even the single word "buckle." (Buckle your belt. The bridge buckles.) M.C. Escher, the great graphic artist, explored the idea visually in many of his symmetry drawings. They act as optical illusions. A dozen white swans swim east across dark waters in strict formation. Blink, and all the dark water becomes twelve identical dark swans in strict formation swimming west, the opposite direction, through white waters which previously were white swans. Look again and all 24 swans swim in opposing motion with not a visible drop of water between them. Wiesel, I suspect, would approve.

In addition to traditional prayers of praise and thanksgiving,

some congregations find a need for the growing body of disso-
nant prayers that simultaneously swim in opposite directions,
that dare enter the "barren land" at twilight where encountering
God is like meeting a "stranger" "by chance." Wiesel territory.
If "Prayer" has appeared in any denominational prayerbook, I
am unaware of it. The text in which it first appeared, *One Generation After*, was published in 1965. Although "Prayer" could well
speak to many more than only *One Generation After*, it is currently out of print. Not so the "poem" selected by François
Mauriac in his Preface to *Night* and quoted here preceding the
section "Wounded Faith."

"Attention must be paid" to one more post-Holocaust prayer,
this written by Wiesel's admired friend, André Schwarz-Bart. It
appears on the last page of his great novel, *The Last of the Just*.
As the penultimate paragraph, it follows a description of execu-
tions by gas chamber with this:

And praised. *Auschwitz*. Be. *Maidanek*. The Lord. *Tre-
Blinka*. And praised. *Buchenwald*. Be. *Mauthausen*. The Lord.
*Belzec*. And praised. *Sobibor*. Be. *Chelmno*. The Lord. *Ponary*.
And praised. *Theresienstadt*. Be. *Warsaw*. The Lord. *Vilna*.
And praised. *Skarzysko*. Be. *Bergen-Belsen*. The Lord. *Janow*.
And praised. *Dora*. Be. *Neuengamme*. The Lord. *Pustkow*.
And praised . . .

(Just 374)

Unlike Wiesel's "Prayer," the above may be too provocative for inclusion in most synagogue prayer books though it does appear in the excellent Martyrology Service included in *The New Mahzor for Rosh Hashonah and Yom Kippur*, 1995. The passage certainly requires a reading with both eyes open, that is, simultaneous praise and horror. Full understanding and acceptance, however, if even possible, may involve for most of us the function of yet a third eye. . . .

About 30 years and many books after *One Generation After*, Wiesel published his memoirs in two volumes: *All Rivers Run to the Sea* and *The Sea Is Never Full*. Both are sources of some previous selections and the following, which is from Volume II. Note especially that the foregoing confession in "Prayer," "I no longer ask You . . . for his faith," is here reconsidered three decades later to read: "I choose to preserve the faith of my childhood." He then asks: "Did I say 'choose'? In truth it is not a real choice." An obvious and yet insightful and honest admission. Not a real choice for Wiesel. Not a real choice for many lifetime observant Jews. It's simply who they are. But for others (including lifetime observant Jews whose religious worlds were shattered beyond repair) and for those Seekers not blessed, or, if you prefer, burdened with a deep childhood immersion in Judaism, the choice for or against faith can indeed be a "real choice," and likely for some a profoundly troubling one.

The writings of Elie Wiesel excel in many areas, but none

more so than in providing testimony to the awesome and perhaps holy attempt of articulating a post-Holocaust position on faith that integrates what has been learned from both sides of the barbed wire fence. Among those who do face the "real choice," however, are readers to whom Wiesel's journey may seem unduly fraught with paradox, intentional contradiction and puzzling encounters with "holy madness." Example: (Man to God) "You want me to cease believing in You . . . In spite of me and in spite of You, I shall shout the Kaddish, which is a song of faith, for You and against You. . . ." (Full quotation in previous section: "Facing Divorce") New readers, unaccustomed to such multilayered outbursts might find them a bit difficult to unravel, let alone digest. More palatable approaches both to and from belief are certainly available. Indeed, with fewer shards of glass. But, take heart. If, as Wiesel claims, "The real tragedy, the real drama, is the drama of the believer," one can reasonably at least begin there. When the believer in question is also a Survivor, his or her testimony or strategies for belief bear an authority, a *gravitas*, deserving special and meticulous attention. Admittedly, those accustomed to the objectivity of searchlights, when limited to light from candles, may experience resistance to the more mystically infused prose. Be patient. It passes.

Granted, Wiesel writes of praise hiding in the heart of blasphemy, of joy beating in the heart of despairing yet defiant Chassidic dance, of a camp prisoner's attempt not to honor but rather to shame God by his accusatory observance of the Yom Kippur fast. An encounter with what he calls the "real drama" includes its weeping God, sometimes in prison, other times disguised as an enemy of His people. Although rooted in tradition, these encounters challenge the limitations of more familiar mainstream-grounded theology. Nevertheless, even candlelight in the right hands can be significantly revealing; on occasion, it can be blinding. *

Are there then truly reasons to "take heart" and in spite of difficulties, pursue his works? Wiesel's rich and original weaving of general, Talmudic, Chassidic learning, lore and personal biography, his belief that an arduous return to devotion is but one of many possibilities to explore, his boldness and his honesty— these qualities alone are sufficient to answer the question. Unless, that is, a full night's sleep is one's desire. In that case, the sardonic observation of I.B. Singer, on being asked why he seldom writes on the Holocaust, says it well: "Jews are people who can't sleep themselves and let nobody else sleep." Including non-

---

* The poet Archibald MacLeish contends that the truth derived from poetry is revealed not within the coupling of disparate images (Beauty and Beast, joyful fury), but rather within the experience which results in the wordless space between them. So too, with variation, the prose of Elie Wiesel. In the "First Person Singular" video quoted previously, he virtually extends the function of juxtaposition to include not only the Coleridgian "balance of discordant qualities" (as in "accusatory praise") but also what amounts to "the space between *any* two words" which he claims "is vaster than the space between Heaven and Hell. To bridge it you must close your eyes and leap. . . ."

believers who understandably turn (or flee) to more appropriate, lucid, and, one assumes, cool-headed proponents of Secular Judaism, Secular Christianity, Secular Humanism, Secular Mountain Climbing with Heavy Boulder, or Ethical Culture and its myriad variations. A restless seeker, acting as one's own shepherd, might pause at the "green pastures" and "still waters" of Psalm 23, beloved by Believers and Secularists alike. The suggestion is conducive to reflection on how differently and how darkly Auschwitz has bloodied those still waters for all, be they wearing black hats, skull caps, shawls, or no head covering at all. Words from survivors stir it again and again.

## MIDSTREAM INTERLUDE

Shortly before his last trip to Auschwitz, this time with the TV personality Oprah Winfrey, Wiesel agreed to an interview with Professor Joseph Lowin of Yeshiva University. They met on February 1, 2006, and the conversation appeared in the March/April issue of *Midstream*. As with most Wiesel interviews, the inevitable question came early and directly.

> **Lowin:** What can you tell [us] about your ongoing struggle with belief?

Wiesel's response was lengthy, but after a few minutes, he summarized:

> **Elie Wiesel:** For me, therefore, it is important to see the whole world through the eyes of a Jew. I say it again and again. I say

it all the time; I choose to identify myself as a Jew. I acknowledge that a Catholic, a Buddhist, or an atheist has the same
right of self-identification.

**Joseph Lowin:** So you flunked Assimilation 101?

**Elie Wiesel:** I never even registered for that course. Some writers
were seduced, but I was never tempted. My problem is not
with Judaism but with humanity. As to my beliefs, people
didn't understand about my faith [in the camps]. I never lost
my faith. If I had lost my faith I would have had no problem.
I don't say I don't have problems with God. I *do* have problems
with God. As I say elsewhere, the tragedy of the believer is
deeper than the tragedy of the non-believer. The non-believer
has a problem with humanity, not with God. We had both. I
did have problems eventually, but not immediately. I stand by
every word in *Night*. In *Night*, I say we condemn God, but
immediately afterward, we went to prayer.

Later, he tells of the *tefillin* (phylacteries) that were smuggled
into the camp and used daily in prayer by his father and himself.

"And what is the prayer we said? 'You have loved us with abundant love.' What kind of prayer was 'abundant love' ? And then
we continued, 'You have pitied us with exceedingly great pity.'
Where is the love? Where is the pity?" (Lowin 5)

Rather than conclude the conversation prematurely, it changes
course to easier topics such as literature, writing in Yiddish,
Hebrew, French and English, such as Israel, world politics, and
his new-found joy as a grandfather.

No word on the private impact of this family blessing, if any, on the "struggle with belief." Many words, however, in his 1999 memoir, on the blessing of music, be it family lullaby or Carnegie Hall cantata, to stir and, on occasion, realign the soul. Case in point: his *"ANI MAAMIN, a Song Lost and Found Again"* discussed here under Stage I of "Mending Faith." The liturgical thrill he once experienced at a Seder upon suddenly remembering and singing the words to *"ANI MAAMIN"* (I Believe) was intensified by its very recall after a thirty year hiatus. As the reverberations of song and spirit receded, the fundamental question returned: "Does this mean I have made peace with God?" (*Sea* 69–70) His response is the body of Declaration III which follows.

## III. DECLARATION III

*"What About My Faith?"*

Does this mean I have made peace with God? I continue to protest His apparent indifference to the injustices that savage His creation. And the Messiah? He should have arrived earlier, much earlier. Perhaps Kafka was right: The Redeemer will come not on the last day but on the day after.

And what about my faith in all that? I would be within my rights to give it up. I could invoke six million reasons to justify my decision. But I don't. I am incapable of straying from the path charted by my ancestors. Without this faith in God, the faith of my father and forefathers, my faith in Israel and in humanity would be diminished. And so I choose to preserve the faith of my childhood.

> It is because I was born a Jew that I can and must choose to be one.
>
> ELIE WIESEL
> . . . To a Young Jew of Today
> (*Generation 164*)

Did I say "choose"? In truth, it is not a real choice. I would not be the man that I am, the Jew that I am, if I betrayed the child who once felt duty-bound to live for God.

I never gave up my faith in God. Even *over there* I went on praying. Yes, my faith was wounded, and still is today. In *Night*, my earliest testimony, I tell of a boy's death by hanging, and conclude that it is God Himself that the killer is determined to murder. I say this from within my faith, for had I lost it I would not rail against heaven. It is because I still believe in God that I argue with Him. As Job said: "Even if He kills me, I shall continue to place my hope in Him." Strange: In secular circles my public statements of faith in God are resented (*Sea* 69–70).

> If He would slay me, I should not hesitate; I should still argue my cause to His face.
>
> JOB 13:15
> New English Bible

Much like the prose Prologue, here retitled "To Be A Jew," the preceding passage from *And the Sea Is Never Full* is especially rich and provocative. I refer to the fourth and last two sentences in the final paragraph.

Regarding the quote from Job: an alternative translation reads: "Though He may slay me, I shall not tremble." Wiesel significantly sides with the version of Job as not only resolute, but hopeful as well. It is a hope conspicuously absent earlier in the paragraph reference to the iconic hanging scene in *Night*.

A variety of interpretations were offered in the Introduction to this monograph. Not quite this one: "In *Night*, my earliest testimony, I tell of a boy's death by hanging, and conclude that it is God Himself that the killer is determined to murder." Dead Jews: not enough; Dead God: Mission accomplished. Strangle the windpipe (God) and the victim (Judaism) will also die. By "God Himself" Wiesel does not intend a euphemism for monotheism or the Jewish Way of Life. By "God Himself" he means God Himself—the identical God he has been wrestling all his adult life. Thus any detachment from God, any loss of faith, by implication diminishes God's recognizable presence in the world. This, as Emil Fackenheim extrapolates and states so eloquently, can tempt (among other causes) "awarding Hitler a posthumous victory." No God equals No Jews equals No Judaism equals "Final Solution" forever.

In a seminal essay, "Jewish Faith and The Holocaust," which first appeared in *Commentary* August (1968), Fackenheim introduced his belief that "a commanding Voice speaks from Auschwitz" and declares, "Jews are forbidden to grant posthumous victories to Hitler." He explains, ". . . In ancient times, the unthinkable Jewish sin was idolatry. Today, it is to respond to Hitler by doing his work" (33). Hitler's work? According to the hanging scene, Hitler's work is killing Jews, Judaism, and, consciously or not, killing the deeply personal God that keeps most Jews Jewish. First, kill the soul. Then the body. And thus the memory. Forever.

A complementary essay entitled "Genesis," by I.B. Singer, approaches the same conclusion when he contrasts the Bible with *Mein Kampf* and claims, "There is no place for these two books in this world. The Hitlers of all nations know that if they want to endure, they have to liquidate the people of the Bible or perish themselves" (Rosenberg 8). So too can there be no room for a law-giving Jehovah in the Third Reich. From this deranged rationale (among many) for liquidating "the people of the Bible," it is a short step to "liquidating" their God. Wiesel witnesses that attempt in *Night*.

The suggestion that it could be, as it were, God Himself gasping for breath in the hangman's noose remains not only shocking but profound. If Hitler is allowed the final victory of virtual deicide in Jewish hearts one could argue, it is tantamount to Jews, through such loss of faith, abandoning their religion and thus becoming Hitler's unwitting accomplices. It is not, however, a matter of belief only. Fackenheim again: Indeed, "A secular Jew cannot make himself believe by a mere act of will, nor can he be commanded to do so; yet he can perform the commandment of Auschwitz" (33). Secular and believing Jews alike must "survive as Jews, lest the Jewish people perish" (32). As we will see at the close of this monograph, Wiesel would likely have little quarrel with this extrapolation and conclusion. In his own words, Wiesel here responds to a relevant question from his interviewer, Richard Heffner, with "If I were to kill the Jew in me, what would I do? I would actually do what Hitler did, on a different scale. And for that and for other reasons, I love my Jewishness" (Heffner 169). And if you were to kill not the Jew but only the God in you, what would you do? Heffner doesn't ask.

Though emphases may differ, the conception of God dying on the gallows, (but not yet dead) remains a sufficiently potent image to reveal the urgency and pathos inherent in Wiesel's refusal ever to let go of Him. If at times his faith, like the dying child, has appeared "hanging by a thread," on examination, the thread invariably proves to be woven of steel. No doing Hitler's work here. Secular Jews who do hear the Commanding Voice of Auschwitz will strike their own bargains with the danger of a "posthumous victory to Hitler." In his preface to the Marion Wiesel translation of NIGHT, Wiesel offers a definition of witness presumably not limited to believers. He or she is one, like himself, ". . . who believes he has a moral obligation to try to prevent the enemy from enjoying one last victory by allowing his crimes to be erased from human memory (VIII)." Wieselian or not, the "Voice" cannot be ignored lightly. Nor can the resentment from others Wiesel experiences in the last sentence of the quotation which opens this section: "In secular circles my public statements of faith in God are resented." More on this in the following "Coda."

---

**And what about God? Once we sang "There is no God like ours," now we sing "There is no God of ours." But we sing. We still sing.**

"THE JEWS"
Yehudah Amichai

---

# CODA

## *For the Beginning Seeker*

### "Greater than the sum . . ."

THE "RESENTMENT IN SECULAR CIRCLES" to Wiesel's affirmations of wounded but constant faith may seem strange to him but inevitable to others. The wounding of faith is understandable, expected, unavoidable. Often, it is deep enough, in fact, to destroy the beliefs of many. But the concomitant tenacity of holding on, of seeking and nurturing a connection (however troubled) to a God his secular audience has virtually erased, can, it seems, easily engender resentment, feelings of intimidation, puzzlement and even begrudged admiration. Some in secular circles may have been survivors themselves. They above all might ask, "How can he still believe?" Wiesel would be the first to understand how many left their souls, let alone their faith, behind those electrified fences. But most did not leave their Judaism. Some assimilationists, yes. Anti-assimilationists, yes. Secular Jews. Some non-synagogue affiliated Zionists. Theologi-

93

cal straddlers (who believe "as if" God were still the fundamental linchpin, the removal of which would cause their religion to unravel). And, if you will, the "Heavy Lifters," Jews like Wiesel, who maintain with no reservation their often wounded but "in spite of" stubborn faith. The list of alternatives goes on and on. Both resentment and tolerance help bind the divisions and subdivisions into a single noisy, contentious Jewish world community.

"If you sought your soul and didn't find a small bird beating home forever where there is no road, You were seeking something else."

DAVID HOPES

What is a Seeker to make of all these choices and quotations? I speak for the quotations only. Some stick. Some don't. Many Wieselian gems are missing. Some maybe should be. Yet, what sounds over simplified or wrong-headed in June may seem profound by winter. An obvious conclusion: the quotations themselves are nervous. They tend to jump around; their relevance often fluctuates with time. Some "favorite lines" can differ as readers age, learn more, forget more, read in different states of mind, moods, etc. Most elusive and yet fortunate: the monograph itself, in its entirety, can possess an influence somehow separate from the sum of its parts.

With patience and slow reading through a distillation of Wiesel's circuitous journey (what Arthur Waskow might call "God-wrestling"), a vague outline of his patterns of thought, his world view, emerges. In time one can almost anticipate responses consistent with his convictions and in so doing, appreciate the integrity and devotion in which those convictions are grounded. Even dissenters agree: Wiesel's subtle balancing of conflicting needs is often of a sufficiently inclusive and intelligent order as to give one pause. More than pause. Once able to sense the overall range and depth of Wiesel's approach, a reader is less inclined to prematurely close the scrapbook over disagreement with this or that quotation. One's personal tally of accept/non-accept quotations is not the point. A conditional trust, born of respect, does not require total agreement; only sufficient patience to withhold outright rejection until the full content and spirit of his words are allowed to simmer and then to do or not to do their work.

The question does not go away. "How can he believe this if he says that?" we ask. I don't know. I do know he is learned, honest and no fool. What then, for example, can careful reading make of these extreme, challenging and recently quoted lines Wiesel gives our forefathers in his cantata *Ani Maamin*: "I believe in You even against Your will—even if You punish me for believing in You . . ."? Faith of such severity is the gift or curse of a precious few. The rest of us may take comfort, however, in the less anguished conclusion of the cantata where blessing comes not from a "silent, absent" God, but from the chorus—arguably made up of fellow humans. The chorus, dispenser of blessing, is reminiscent of the God Wiesel elsewhere claims can be found "in simple human relationships" (*Hope Against Hope* interview). My point: cultivating a feel for "the whole" reveals the inclusive nature of Wiesel's work which might be overlooked in a scrap-book that necessarily spotlights only "the parts."

> Anybody with an active mind lives on tentatives rather than on tenets. You've got to feel a certain pleasure in the tentativeness of it all, the unfinality of it.
>
> FROST

So too with his critics. Consider what at first appears to be a rather dismissive observation: [In *Ani Maamin*] "Wiesel has suggested a majestic, consoling image of God in tears who is grateful to the Jews for their unmerited faith. Yet this image leads us to question whether there can be any difference between a silent absent God whose empathy is imperceptible to man, and no God at all" (Berenbaum 127). A seeker of paths into belief might hastily imagine a door slamming. One more seasoned in the vagaries of quotations out of context and one possessing a sense of Wiesel's world beyond the sum of quotations might see how Wiesel could agree with his critic. As with our examination of his twelve-sentence "Prayer," there are here at least two ways to describe Wiesel's God. Yes, one seems to contradict the other. However, the "majestic consoling image of God" could well satisfy the believer, whereas the "silent absent God" description (which could also describe "no God at all") might reach to and intrigue, if not totally engage the searching doubter. After all, Berenbaum's description works both ways. That is, if God seems silent and His empathy imperceptible to man, the ensuing possibly false conclusion of "no God at all" may be due to man's deficiencies in listening and perceiving. So it goes. In any event, both believer and doubter can find in this inclusive rendering of the same God concept that to which he or she, at that moment, can individually relate and begin to refine.

The "parts" (individual quotations) can change relevance with time and circumstance. The sum (overall impression of entire monograph) provides a more direct, general and trustworthy insight to at least the shifting contours of the author's mind. The "whole" allows a glimpse of how the parts might inform, interact, and generally impact the author's way of understanding the world, his sensibility and, by extension, how they may do so (one would think) for the sensibilities of his more religiously inclined readers. Passing the sparks. Although the individual words are often forgotten, their force nevertheless has, does, and, one hopes, will continue to fuel and enrich the quest of seekers regardless of religious or secular inclinations.

The whole, in this case, is indeed greater than the sum of its parts.

It just needs to cook.

> . . . Since someone will forever be surprising
> A hunger in himself to be more serious,
> And gravitating with it to this ground,
> Which, he once heard, was proper to grow wise in
> If only that so many dead lie around.
> —Philip Larkin

# Conclusion

## "The Madman's Prayer"

THERE IS NO DENYING a few entries in the foregoing scrapbook yield somewhat conflicting conclusions. If they share
one conviction it is the against-all-odds invincibility of Wiesel's
transcendent faith. He has been steadfast, nay, relentless, in his
acceptance of and need for relationship with a God however
unknowable, wearing one mask or many. Though his God may
appear loving or punishing, mighty or helpless, intimate or, yes,
indifferent, for him God is always there. Not so for all. God's
apparent absence in the face of genocide, though incomprehensible, is for some nevertheless evil of such magnitude it thus
becomes the final cause, on moral grounds, to reject God outright.
(Admittedly out of context, these four lines from Jacob Glatstein's
"Dead Men Don't Praise God" capture the fury: "We received the
Torah on Sinai/ and in Lublin we gave it back/ Dead men don't
praise God/ The Torah was given to the living" (Glatstein 68).
(The title, with different emphasis, is from Psalm 115).

Notwithstanding the history of such arguments, this specific outrage is obviously responsible for many current questioners to not only reject but also doubt God's very existence. (The writer Gore Vidal claims he is a "born-again atheist.") We can imagine neither position embraced within Wiesel's world view. Yet, among those Jews driven to these conclusions or to a variation of secular leanings, Wiesel is respectful and most likely approving of those who nevertheless persevere in their Jewish affiliation. His words: "Even if they are agnostic, they have the right to call themselves Jews and Jewish thinkers" (Cheron 163). At the same time, he is predictably distressed though understanding of those who do not.

> **To be or not to be**
> **That is the question.**
>
> HAMLET
>
> **To be and not to be**
> **That is the answer.**
>
> HERBERT GOLD

This litany of quotations, however, can conclude with the certainty that Wiesel is not seeking personal membership in Rabbi Sherwin Wine's Institute for Secular Humanist Judaism. Nor is he willing to posit, as had his colleague, Rabbi Richard Rubenstein, that "omnipotent Nothingness is Lord of all creation." It is a definition that may satisfy a determined Sisyphus with his mountain and boulder, his freedom from hope and his acceptance of a universe perceived as both Godless and absurd. Sisyphus trudges bravely, defiantly, honorably, but alone. . . . and with no prayer on his lips. May the "bread of indifference on which he feeds his greatness" (Camus) nourish him well.

As we have seen, Wiesel's fate is equally daunting. He too is no stranger to late-night encounters with the existential Absurd, though they may lack the pristine clarity of rock, mountain, cloudless and empty sky. Consider burdens of searing memories and soul-crushing losses, Auschwitz, an "inability" to reject God, a witness to the world of God and God's absence. Add the accomplishment of a unique devotion to God made radical not by suppression but rather by its insistence on holding fast to the very barbed wire which often disallows devotion in others. An achievement even Sisyphus might not scorn. Unlike Sisyphus, however, only rarely does Wiesel "walk alone" (and even then with paradox and with Torah).

> The wall is silent.
> I speak for it,
> blessing myself.
> DAVID IGNATOW
>
> . . . and like David
> I bless myself
> with all my might.
> SAMUEL MENASHE
>
> . . . for everything
> flowers from within,
> of self-blessing;
> GALWAY KINNELL

Again, where does that leave us? With a caveat. Dividing Wiesel's words into four convenient stages of "mending" or "healing" faith is useful but not fundamental, both helpful and deceptive. It is not Wieselian. No 12-step program here. His tales do not usually conclude in a Stage IV glow of tentative reconciliation, let alone compassion for God's "tears" last

> Mensh Tracht und
> Gott Lacht.
> (Man plans and God
> laughs.)

seen in Stage I. Often they conclude where they began: at dusk. We began with the gallows in *Night*. Then on to "Just Man of Sodom," "Sisyphus" and "The Fatman" who could not stop eating. (He who prepared his body for immolation as an act of futile protest and, some claim, as a means to force God's attention.) We now end with the same haunting theme but in mysterious reverse: "The Jews Who Prayed too Loudly." In his book *God's Presence In History*, previously quoted, the philosopher and theologian Emil Fackenheim, titles the story "The Madman's Prayer," and reports: " The writer Elie Wiesel tells the story of a small group of Jews who were gathered to pray in a little synagogue in Nazi-occupied Europe. As the service went on, suddenly a pious Jew who was slightly mad—for all pious Jews were by

**To believe and not to believe. Is that the answer?**

then slightly mad—burst in through the door. Silently he listened for a moment as the prayers ascended. Slowly he said: "Shh, Jews! Do not pray so loud! God will hear you. Then He will know that there are still some Jews left alive in Europe" (p. 67).

Of all the masks God has worn in this somewhat arbitrary scrapbook of quotations, one has remained off-limits. *Ani Maamin* raised the "what if" possibility of God punishing His people for believing in Him, whereas here we have the conviction, actually believed by the madman, that God is out to kill Jews. Even if he speaks only for himself, his warning does not urge an immolation to arouse the heavens as does the Fatman's tale. Nor does he plead that they abandon the prayer books to run and hide where they might not so attract God's attention. Instead, the congregation is cautioned to continue their evening prayers, connecting to God, yet at the same time, in order not to be heard by the very God so addressed, to pray softly.

With apologies to Job ("Though He slay me, yet will I trust Him"), may one presume an alternative response implied by the tale's frantic messenger: "Though He actually slay my people and I can no longer trust Him, yet will I therefore whisper my prayers but too quietly for Him to hear"? Quietly, almost as our silence upon encountering such tortured, such holy defiance.

> The edge is
> what I have
> —THEODORE ROETHKE

If the achievement of radical devotion is a prerequisite for admission to the proverbial "inner circle" of our title, I have argued for Wiesel's honorary membership. In fact, I would now urge his chair be placed, if not close, at least near to that very latest of pious madmen, he who warns, "Shhh, not so loud." Two resolute believers in a God Who, when most needed, can appear to them as tragically negligent, if not at times malignant. A God in Whom they nevertheless refuse to abandon belief in either His existence or His human involvement however tenuous, however puzzling that belief, especially to the nonreligious mind. Whereas traditional belief in God as well as faith in prayer, sung or whispered, may sometimes be elusive and unpredictable within this gathering, DEVOTION is not. It is the common denominator uniting them with an audacious and hard-won conviction which emphasized bedrock loyalty perhaps far more than the quality of devotion implying worshipful love. In spite of silent skies, corroding doubts and latent fury . . . they simply will not let go. The mere suggestion of surrender, letting go of one's unique historic identity and its core belief of one God in exchange for—as viewed by the Circle majority—a voluntary post-Holocaust assimilation would be the plea for an act, both profane and a desecration.

The pleas for prayers too soft to be heard (and admittedly mad) can predictably seem much too loud to the more rational "no nonsense" Seeker. In defense of the plea's indifference to legitimate charges of making no logical sense, a Wieselian response might offer the cryptic "No sense? Of course not. So be it." Traditional cause and effect reasoning apparently is viewed as a luxury irrelevant in a universe already gone mad. In spite of no training in Kabbalah and no reference to Holocaust prayer, the Welsh poet, Dylan Thomas, for his own reasons, chants: "When logics die/ The secret of the soil/ Grows through the eye/ and blood jumps in the sun." Although we have considered these issues under sections HOLY MADNESS and PARADOX, a brief and final pause at Carnegie Hall is in order. Once more, if you will, let us reconsider our verse from the *Ani Maamin* cantata (*Mending Faith*: Stage I, p.21–23) which also forces the limits of devotion to near its border where logics die as revolt and possibly madness awaken. A wilderness most Seekers need never personally tread.

The silent, inexplicable God imagined in "The Madman's Prayer" and the confounding Patriarch's words which here fol-

low from Wiesel's cantata are not the stuff of conventional discourse or of abbreviated prayer books. They are indeed
provocative post-Holocaust challenges to familiar, "rational,"
and compartmentalized expressions of belief
and devotion. Yet the Patriarch's cantata
response (like whispered prayers) essentially
transforms both belief and devotion into
intentional acts of righteous disobedience and

> **My soul, like some heat-maddended fly Keeps buzzing at the sill.**
>
> **THEODORE ROETHKE**

thus, for some, confirms their undying utility and power.
Observe his words again: "I believe in You/ Even against Your
will/ Even if You punish me/ For believing in You." Absurd? So
be it. Devotion *in extremis*? Hyperbolic? Metaphoric? Meaningful? Inspirational? Heroic? A quandary reminiscent of pushing a
boulder up an endless mountain.

Devotion once stripped of complacency and emboldened with
pious rebellion somehow survives beyond the impulse for rational behavior and beyond the need to ask God's favor ("Even
against Your will"). Wiesel once stated in a 1994 YMHA interview: "I say to God: You don't deserve Your people. But Your
people still pray to You". (Shalom TV, May 2008) Their words,
however, likely bear no resemblance to Wiesel's 1965 unforgettable "Prayer," written now in his own voice and free of expected
supplication as examined earlier in these pages. (Since quotations
removed from context often run the danger of distortion, the
determined Seeker might reconsider them, when possible, in the

setting from which they came. In this instance, see Section "Prayer," pp. 74–81). Although the "Prayer" ends somewhat conciliatory, the rage is both controlled and severe: "I no longer ask You for either rest or wisdom/ . . . Love, love is not Yours to give." At the core of this contentious devotion, almost consumed by fire, still burns the familiar, steadfast refusal at any cost to let go of God. Not "rational." Not negotiable. Not for everyone. But pure. Distilled in fact to an inviolate and profound allegiance which flows more from bone than from heart, a choice observed above in the Inner Circle. A choice that perhaps is not a choice at all.

Measured against either high-decibel wrath or robust choirs of praise, that inward denial of surrender, a refusal to turn away from God may sometimes sound by contrast a quiet voice, on occasion quiet as a whisper in "The Madman's Prayer." Pure, rare, as captured by Wiesel, but of variable intensities, a personal loyalty though grievously challenged yet tenaciously rooted in God which, when even spoken softly, can reveal the passion of a cantoral cry. Atheists and believers who, on moral grounds, feel no such loyalty to an "absent" (let alone "malignant") God, but rather a conscientious compulsion to reject Him altogether are respectfully exempt from this stubborn yet exclusive congregation. (Had they been offered membership, it would have been summarily refused.) Their spiritual identities must be nourished elsewhere. So too, respectfully honored though exempt from this

Circle, are those of non-Holocaust-related and unquestioned loyalty to God; a fidelity yet vital, holy and deeply felt as that instinctively lavished on family, on one's own people.

Believers, however, who reach even a portion of the authentic, fractured and multilayered Devotion (rare, purified, fine-tuned, Wieselian or worthy versions thereof) may find themselves in prayer, as anticipated in the

> **"... the experience of mixed exaltation and horror ..."**
>
> **ROBERT GRAVES**

Introduction, with "both eyes open." The image is there followed by this quotation from Wiesel: "To thank Him for Jerusalem and not question Him for Treblinka is hypocrisy." There may be many reasons short of hypocrisy why one might not question a so-conceived silent or absent God. Yet the hunger for answers from a Creator deemed worthy of gratitude can be relentless. Some non-questioners with faith intact accept Treblinka as well as Jerusalem as man-made expressions of the innate, tragic yet evolving "human condition." God is absolved of responsibility. Others see a devolution, a Sisyphian challenge which calls forth, even if hopeless, a quest for Answers from Above. The act of questioning becomes one of implied accusation and of allegiance. Wiesel might add: an act of self respect.

How far then from geographic and metaphorical Treblinka to Jerusalem? The Pilot can answer in flight miles. The Poet hopes to capture truths (otherwise unavailable) residing in the tension, the space close or vast separating such juxtaposed poles. Rarely so close, however, as visioned by Mystics who seek not separation but the exceptional merging of opposites, in this instance joy and fury, which can occur when polar opposites become one. Consider now such fusion as portrayed in Section 4, Part 1 of *The Gates of the Forest.*

> Crows want everything black. Owls want everything white.
>
> W.M. BLAKE

Does not the metaphoric absence of God at Treblinka at least inhibit the religious impulse of gratitude for Jerusalem? No, according to the Rebbe in Wiesel's novel. Rather one feeds the other: "There is joy as well as fury in the Hasid's dancing . . . [referring to God]." "You've taken away every reason for singing, but I shall sing." "Even louder," he might add (p. 196, also "Stage III discussion). Holy dances which embrace this dichotomy can be as a touchstone, a daring beacon for prayer. Jerusalem and Treblinka co-exist. Not only next to but virtually inside each other. Protest through joy. Two realities; yin/yang. One tension. One prayer. André Schwartz-Bart's *The Last of the Just* with this jolting and yet appropriate reprise: "And praised. Auschwitz. Be. Majdanek. The Lord. Treblinka. . . ." A related litany is sung in Wiesel's cantata as discussed in *Mending Faith*/Stage 1: "I believe, Abraham, despite Treblinka. I believe, Isaac, Because of Belsen. I believe, Jacob, Because and in spite of Majdanek." (*Ani Maamin*) The contrast here between writers is telling. . . .

Others will argue that regardless of how close or how distant the God-centered juxtapositions (be they joy-fury, Praised . . .

Be . . . The Lord-Auschwitz, Jerusalem-Treblinka), no matter how insightful, inspiring, eternal, or how puzzling, brutal, useless, the impulse to not only challenge them but when appropriate to "question Him" burns even more deeply. "Wisdom to accept that which is beyond our understanding" is partial wisdom only. The questions, ancient and more current than Treblinka can become desperate. Jobian. For the faithful-questions more threatening to belief. "Whose mad creation is this?" For the secular Humanist the absence of a personal Creator becomes more obvious. For the Inner Circle itself, issues surrounding God's power and "arbitrary" compassion remain constant as prayer.

Indeed, the usual discord among these resolute believers is not one of fundamental faith against doubt but rather possibilities of Chassidic joy enclosed within actual fury at the same God. Not contrasts of belief against (however persuasive) non-belief but rather dissension for example on the Schwartz-Bart "and praised . . . Be . . . The Lord," which in context is a prayer possibly intended for consolation moments before the killing showers. Why then is it juxtaposed with locations of the crematoria? Locations from which praise of God, if uttered at least today, would seem intentionally blasphemous. And so it is.

As for the juxtaposition of Jerusalem and Treblinka, the issue of Inner Circle controversy again questions not God's existence but rather the rationale regarding man's capacity for such evil and God's related judgment as to whom He does and does not forsake. The space between our holy Jerusalems and profane Treblinkas still churns, especially for those of religious disposition, with the venerable tensions of Theodicy; the defense of God in view of the existence of evil. Hence the trouble soul of this legacy. Primal, apparently irreconcilable, be it questioned (how could a loving God allow . . . ?) or be it tolerated in silence. Both responses can remain grounded in belief either within or without a religious setting. Were an answer from Above forthcoming, as Wiesel reminds us elsewhere in this meditation, he would reject it. So too would many others who share his values though not necessarily his beliefs.

> I said, "Is it good friend?" "It is bitter,—bitter" he answered "But I like it because it is bitter and because it is my heart."
> STEPHEN CRANE

The conflict between despair and faith, symbolized by Treblinka and Jerusalem, defies final resolution. We do well to embrace the existential tension which results. Its value lies in expressing with clarity and honesty one of many permanent, inexplicable and defining components of our human (and inhuman) condition. At the same time, this is "partial wisdom" only and does not imply surrender to madness nor mere complacency. Religious tensions born of conflicting polarities incorporate but are not always limited by them. . . . There can be room for something new to evolve. Poets lead the way. And wise storytellers. We have previously considered juxtaposition from Wiesel's more intriguing efforts: "holy madness," "accusatory praise," "joyful fury." However, to reconcile the endurance of suffering and evil in an all-powerful, merciful, God-centered universe finally may require the vision of a yet-to-be-born Copernicus. Legacies die hard.

The choice of silent acceptance, brave or foolish, we have seen indisputably is not for Wiesel. Better an answer he rejects than no answer at all. His warning to bypass what he calls hypocrisy (which is "not question Him") naturally becomes a call to instead "question Him for Treblinka": a forthright spontaneous reaction sanctioned by a vigorous biblical tradition of protest. In spite of Divine silence and notwithstanding gratitude for Jerusalem, interrogators who respond to the call to question Him yet fully expecting no reply [man does not hear God] may find comfort, such as it is, in the company of those urged to pray only in whispers [God does not hear man]. As previously discussed, with prayers too soft to be heard, according to the madman's deranged plan, God would then be unable to locate the source of prayers, thus freeing the devoted from His assumed wrath. Be it sanity and/or madness, that perceived as Divine silence does not preclude the persistence of a believer's need for answers. If hopeless—yet honorable. Why no rescue? Why no Covenant? Why then Jerusalem? Why no response?. . . Why must one Remember? To question God's absence or possible complicity in human trauma is not entirely futile. It does recharge Holocaust memory and one's consequent resolutions. It does help retard the individual and generational encroachment of forgetfulness.

The well-documented facts of Treblinka, as with those of Auschwitz and other Death Factories, are sufficiently horrendous to, one hopes, never be erased from consciousness. The very pain of those memories, however, are known to also have a reverse effect. Though seemingly unforgettable, pain can reduce the frequency and intensity of recall while the dust of decades and generations of separation increase. As for Jerusalem, the Psalms leave no doubt: "If I forget thee, o Jerusalem, may my right hand lose its cunning." A now updated warning continues: [If I forget thee, o Treblinka. . . . ] may my tongue cleave to the roof of my mouth." (cf. Psalm 137) Wiesel's own metaphor, which calls forth "the very salt of man," describes also the men and women who protect the content and through "custom and ceremony" sustain the guardians of those memories for which there are so many words and yet no adequate words at all.

**How but in custom and ceremony Are innocence and beauty born?**
W.B. YEATS

In light of the endless afflictions suffered upon the Jewish People, it has been said that God spared them one: Amnesia. Holocaust remembrance indeed is woven in dark threads though sporadically throughout various prayerbooks. This is most evident in the "Martyrology" selections reserved for New Year services and the also annual Holocaust Day commemorations. Flames from the furnaces of Treblinka, once recalled with or without

Jerusalem, can still roar with the pain of memory as recent as two to three generations. A sacred trust. Pain and fury. At perpetrators, at witnesses, at the silent who turned away and inevitably including the One under present inquiry Whom, at the risk of hypocrisy we tend "not to question for Treblinka. . . ." To question can involve not only tortuous remembrance, painful accusation, a response of apparent silence and toleration of the intolerable. Mysteriously, it can also ignite Inner Circle refusal to let go of God,

> Because I remember, I despair.
> Because I remember, I have the duty to reject despair.
>
> —WIESEL

resulting allegiance often fueled by repressed rebellion ("I believe in You even against Your will") and in Wiesel's case, perhaps something more. (Is there not yet a Yiddish proverb claiming a touch of hypocrisy may actually be good for the soul?)

A fundamental loyalty to God among seasoned members of the Inner Circle remains by definition its common denominator. With or without Wiesel's writings therein would thrive an indigenous compulsion to question their assumed Creator. As with the juxtaposition encounters, no challenge is intended to or ultimately capable of permanently separating them from God. Yet their devotion is not blind. Their prayers, for some, are not conciliatory. Their allegiance, though invincible, is not forgiveness. To modify a line from "Prayer": nor is it "Love? Love is not Yours [or perhaps theirs] to give. . . ."

> "... it is the fear of the Lord That is the beginning of wisdom."
>
> LEON KASS

As true with Radical Devotion itself, forgiveness and love of

God ("Thou shalt love the Lord thy God with all thy heart, with all thy soul and with all thy might. . . .") may be noble and worthy quests although hardly attainable by everyone. For many, yes. Among others are those who, between episodic bouts of fury, could ask "from whence then may ever cometh" the requisite resolve to offer God, if much less than total absolution, at least restoration of my once whispered reverence? In addition are believers, including those torn by ambivalence and now also beyond the Inner Circle, who might wish for similar guidance. Mindful of joy co-mingled with fury in Chassidic dance, they seek help enabling their own less combustible chemistry. It is simply for expressing awe co-mingled with offering gratitude for personal and all other perceived blessings. The issue is not one of familiar healing. It is one of familiar offering and questioning through prayer the conflicted longing for a "Protector." Why conflicted? Only when the longing is entwined with rage and wariness against One Who when most needed can (conceivably, apparently, heartbreakingly) respond with what amounts to "looking the other way."

Where then to find such transformative counsel? For Wiesel, no such intermediaries . . . one Source only: "I ask You what I might ask a stranger met by chance at twilight in a barren land" ("Prayer"). A setting significantly not conducive to expressions of loyalty, reverence, awe, gratitude. A landscape presumably not far from the outskirts of Treblinka—or could that in the distance be Jerusalem? The double guidance he seeks therein nevertheless dares to delve more deeply even than many gathered with him in that imaginary Circle would care to go: "God of Abraham, Isaac and Jacob, enable me to forgive You and enable the child I once was to forgive me too. I no longer ask You for the life of that child, nor even for his faith. . . . (cf. Section PRAYER)

What more is there to say?

Remembrance . . . Question.

Accusation . . . Rebellion.

Allegiance . . . Toleration. . . .

Yet Wiesel despairs: "Enable me to forgive You. . . ."

The prayer in entirety remains an enigmatic, haunting demonstration of Radical Devotion by a writer whose comfort with paradox (God as potentially both enabler and recipient of the same forgiveness) is exceeded only by his boldness, desperation and honesty.

Near his eightieth birthday, on reviewing the quotations selected for this commentary, Elie Wiesel wrote: "The theme of faith that is at the center of your monograph is also at the

> **A Wounded Deer
> leaps highest—
> I've heard the
> Hunter tell—**
> —EMILY DICKINSON 165

center of my life. As you understand, all questions must remain open. . . ." (Addendum).

Even in prayer. So be it.

*Personal Disclosure: Were I able to fully appreciate the depth of fidelity as demonstrated in these pages (or to trust it in others) . . .*

*Were I able to more wisely probe the anatomy of belief and of doubt, be they centered in brain, heart, bone, blood, gene, this Meditation perhaps would have never been assembled nor remain necessary.*

The depth, the meaning,
The very salt of man is
His constant desire to ask
The question even deeper
Within himself, to feel even
More intimately the existence
Of an unknowable answer.

—*Town 176*

. . . as if to say: You, God, do not want me to be Jewish; Well, Jewish we shall be nevertheless, despite Your will.

E.W. JUDAISM
Summer 1967

# Addenda

## I. PUZZLE

What's green, hangs on
walls and whistles?

A herring!

But a herring doesn't hang
on walls, whistle or is green.

Sooo, you paint it green.

But it still doesn't hang on walls.

So you buy a nail and hang
it on the wall.

But even green and on a wall,
a herring doesn't whistle.

So, It Doesn't Whistle . . .

*thanks to Jacob Zimmerman*

## II. SOLUTION

When the great Rabbi Israel
Baal Shem-Tov saw misfortune
threatening the Jews it was
his custom to go into a certain
part of the forest to meditate.
There he would light a fire,
say a special prayer, and the
miracle would be accomplished
and the misfortune averted.

Later, when his disciple, the
celebrated Magid of Mezritch,
had occasion, for the same
reason, to intercede with heaven,
he would go to the same
place in the forest and say:
"Master of the Universe, listen!
I do not know how to light the fire,
but I am still able to say the prayer."
and again the miracle would
be accomplished.

Still later, Rabbi Moshe-Leib
Of Sasov, in order to save his
People once more, would go into
the forest and say: "I do not know
how to light the fire, I do not

know the prayer, but I know the
place and this must be sufficient."
It was sufficient and the
miracle was accomplished.

Then it fell to Rabbi Israel
of Rizhyn to overcome misfortune.
Sitting in his armchair, his head
In his hands, he spoke to God:
"I am unable to light the fire
and I do not know the prayer;
I cannot even find the place
In the forest. All I can do
Is to tell the story, and
This must be sufficient."
And it was sufficient.

*—THE GATES OF THE FOREST*

## III.  SUMMARY

**CONFESSIONS OF A MARGINAL JEW**

Lord
I speak to You after a long silence.
Auschwitz between us.

Because
we are unlike them
they destroy us.
We are unlike them
because
of You.

In our silence
they hear surrender.
And that is why
I must speak
Your
Name.

Should our lips ever again . . ,

(after midnight petals
secretly
unfold to the moon)

Should our voices open once more into
wordless melodies of praise,
On that day
the Curse
will be
stilled.

But tonight is not for singing;

Only

gunfire in Warsaw

(With the tip of a rifle
our children, possessed
carved tablets into moist cellar walls:

"Thou Shall Not
Surrender")

and a whispered prayer

(my head does not bow
my knees do not bend)
For the dead who are beyond all mercy

For the dead . . . Lord,
and for

You.

—Michael Ritzen

# Works Cited

## Works by Elie Wiesel

*A Jew Today*
New York: Random, 1979
Vintage Books

*The Accident*
Toronto: Collins, 1985
Hill and Wang

*All Rivers Run to the Sea*
New York: Knopf, 1994

*And the Sea Is Never Full*
New York: Alfred A. Knopf, 1999

*The Gates of the Forest*
Holt, 1966
Avon Books

*Legends of Our Time*
Holt, 1968
Avon Books

*Messengers of God*
New York: Random, 1977
Pocket Book

*Night*
New York: Hill and Wang, 2006

*One Generation After*
New York: Random, 1965

*The Six Days of Destruction*
Wiesel and Friedlander
Paulist Press, 1988

*"The Solitude of God"*
Lecture: 92nd St. Y
New York, October 31, 1985
(reprinted in Rittner)

*Souls on Fire*
New York: Random, 1972

*The Town Beyond the Wall*
Schocken Books, 1982

*The Trial of God*
Schocken Books, 1986


## Secondary Sources

Berenbaum, Michael. *Elie Wiesel: God, The Holocaust and the Children of Israel*
New Jersey: Behrman House, 1979

Borowitz, Eugene B. *Choices in Modern Jewish Thought*
New Jersey: Behrman House, 1995

Boschert-Kimmig and Schuster. *Hope Against Hope*
  Paulist Press, 1999
  A Stimulus Book

Camus. Albert. *The Myth of Sisyphus*
  New York: Random House, 1955
  Vantage Books

Cargas, Harry James, ed. *Responses to Elie Wiesel*
  New York: Persea Books, 1978

Cargas, Harry James. *Harry James Cargas in Conversation with Elie Wiesel*
  New York: Paulist Press, 1976

de Saint Cheron. *Evil and Exile*
  University of Notre Dame Press, 2000

Dubois, Marcel. "The Memory of Self and the Memory of God"
  Reprinted in *Elie Wiesel Between Memory and Hope*
  *Carol Rittner, ed. p. 67*

Fackenheim, Emil. *God's Presence in History*
  New York University Press, 1970

Fackenheim, Emil. "Jewish Faith and the Holocaust"
  *Commentary*, August 1968 (30–36)

Freedman, Samuel. "Bearing Witness: The Life and Work of Elie Wiesel"
  *The New York Times Magazine*, October 23, 1983

Glatstein, Jacob. *The Selected Poems of Jacob Glatstein*
  New York: October House, 1972

Heffner, Richard D. *Conversations with Elie Wiesel*
New York: Schocken Books, 2001

Knopp, Josephine. *"Wiesel and the Absurd"*
Reprinted in *Responses to Elie Wiesel*, Harry J. Cargas, ed.
New York: Persea Books, 1978

Kolatch, Alfred. *What Jews Say About God*
New York: Jonathan David, 1999

Kolitz, Zvi. *Yossel Rakover Speaks to God*
Holocaust Challenges to Religious Faith
New Jersey: KTAV Publishing House, 1995

Lowin, Joseph. "A Conversation with Elie Wiesel"
*Midstream*, April, 2006 (4–7)

Morgan, Michael L. *Beyond Auschwitz*
New York: Oxford University Press, 2001

O'Connor. *A Journey of Faith: Conversations with John Cardinal O'Connor*
D. Fine, 1990

Rosenberg, David, ed. *Congregation*
Harcourt, 1987

Roth and Berenbaum, eds. *Holocaust: Religious and Philosophical Implications*
New York: Paragon House, 1989

Schwarz-Bart, André. *The Last of the Just*
New York: Atheneum, 1961

Sherwin, Byron. "Elie Wiesel and Jewish Theology"
Reprinted in *Responses to Elie Wiesel*, Harry J. Cargas, ed.
New York: Persea Books, 1978

# Professional Acknowledgments

We acknowledge the following publishers:

ALL RIVERS RUN TO THE SEA and THE SEA IS NEVER FULL by
Elie Wiesel.
Copyright 1999. Random House, Inc.
A JEW TODAY by Elie Wiesel. Copyright 1978. Random House, Inc.
NIGHT by Elie Wiesel. Copyright 2006. Farrar, Straus & Giroux
THE ACCIDENT by Elie Wiesel. Copyright 1972. Farrar, Straus &
Giroux
THE GATES OF THE FOREST by Elie Wiesel. ©
English Language Translation by Frances Frenaye. Copyright 1966
by Henry Holt & Co. Reprinted by permission of Henry Holt &
Co., LLC
SOULS ON FIRE by Elie Wiesel. Copyright 1962. Random House, Inc.

## Secondary Sources

Benenbaum, Michael. ELIE WIESEL: GOD, THE HOLOCAUST AND
THE CHILDREN OF ISRAEL © 1979 Behrman House, Inc.
Borowitz, Eugene B. CHOICES IN MODERN JEWISH THOUGHT ©
1995 Behrman House, Inc.
Boschert-Kimmig & Schuster. HOPE AGAINST HOPE © 1999 A
Stimulus Book
Cargas, Harry James. HARRY JAMES CARGAS in CONVERSATION
with ELIE WIESEL © 1976 New York: Paulist Press
deSaint Cheron. EVIL and EXILE © 2000 University of Notre Dame
Press
Dubois, Marcel. "The memory of Self and the Memory of God"
Reprinted in ELIE WIESEL: BETWEEN MEMORY and HOPE ©
1990
Carol Rittner, ed. New York University Press

Fackenheim, Emil. "Jewish Faith and the Holocaust"
COMMENTARY, August 1968 (See GOD'S PRESENCE IN
HISTORY)

Kolatch, Alfred. WHAT JEWS SAY ABOUT GOD © 1999 New York:
Jonathan David Pub.

Lowin, Joseph. "A Conversation With Elie Wiesel" © 2006
MIDSTREAM, April, '06

Roth & Brenenbaum, eds. HOLOCAUST: RELIGIOUS &
PHILOSOPHICAL IMPLICATIONS © 1989 New York: Paragon
House

Sherwin, Byron. "Elie Wiesel & Jewish Theology" reprinted in
RESPONSES TO ELIE WIESEL, Harry Cargas, ed. New York:
Persea Books © 1978